The Book of Needlepoint Stitches

Susan Higginson

The Book of Needlepoint Stitches

Abbooks

A & C Black · London

First published in 1989 by
A & C Black (Publishers) Limited
35 Bedford Row, London WC1

ISBN 0 7136 3146 5

A CIP catalogue record for this book
is available from the British Library

Printed in Great Britain by BPCC Paulton Books Limited
Typeset by Susan Higginson.

All line drawings by the author.
Photography by the author and Alphabet & Image Ltd.

Front cover stitches, each row, left to right:
leaf variation, upright cross, diamond eyelet, basketweave tent
wheel, scallop, petal, French knots on stalks
web, graduated sheaf, diagonal fly, Hungarian diamond
single trammed Gobelin, Norwich, leaf, spider's web
satin petal, jacquard, satin square, Brighton.

Acknowledgements

I should like to thank my family for their interest and
encouragement during the writing of this book, also my
students for their enthusiasm and willingness to invent
new stitches, two of which — snowflake by Beryl Judd and a
leaf variation by Sheila Brown — are included. Many thanks
also to Alphabet & Image Ltd., Sherborne, without whom this
book could never have appeared in its present form.
I should like to dedicate this book to my father and mother.

Contents

1. Introduction   6

2. Materials and Techniques   7

3. Choosing a Design   11

4. Stitches   12

    ⊞ Straight   12
    ☒ Crossed   40
    ◉ Eyelet   53
    ⊻ Pile   57
    ♣ Leaf   59
    ◩ Diagonal   63
    ∝ Looped   88
    ✳ Motif   90
    Ж Tied   99
    ❀ Knot   104

5. List of stitches by type   110

6. Alphabetical list of stitches   111

7. Bibliography and suppliers   112

Introduction

Many people who enjoy doing needlepoint, also called tapestry or canvas work, use only one stitch and do not realise the wealth of other stitches they could add to their repertoire. How much more could they enjoy their craft if they experimented with some of the tens of different stitches illustrated here.

None of them is at all difficult (especially as the diagrams are all numbered to show order of stitching, and successive rows of stitches are shown with bars of varying thickness), many of them are delightfully chunky and three-dimensional and most are larger than tent or half cross stitch, thus covering the canvas more quickly. A piece of needlepoint using a wide variety of stitches has a sculptural quality quite lacking in one made with only one stitch, and is much more interesting to look at.

This directory makes no claims to being exhaustive — there are after all over three hundred needlepoint stitches if you count variations. What I have collected together are the stitches my students and I have found most useful and attractive during many years of needlepoint. There are also several stitches which are completely new, having been made up by myself or one of my students to meet some special need.

All the stitches are shown in colour as it is so difficult to get the feel of an essentially colourful medium if it is only illustrated in black and white.

Several completed pieces of needlepoint are included in the book, annotated and with sections shown in close-up to demonstrate how some of the stitches may be used.

I hope this book will inspire many needlepoint enthusiasts, who have previously worked only with kits, to design their own canvases. There is a great deal of satisfaction to be had in seeing a project through right from the first idea, and the hints and tips included with each stitch about where it may best be used should help with design ideas.

Materials & Techniques

MATERIALS

Needlepoint does not require much in the way of specialised materials or equipment, so as a great deal of time and effort will go into producing a finished item, it is worth while using the best materials available. Here are some guidelines to help you to know what you need.

Canvas: There is a bewildering variety of canvas on the market, but basically two different types are made — single thread or mono canvas and double thread or Penelope canvas, both available in a number of different mesh sizes.

Choose a double thread canvas only if you want to tram your work (see Tramming stitch), to give it extra strength and thickness, or if you want to be able to divide the double mesh in certain areas to form a smaller single mesh enabling you to show great detail.

Choose the size of mesh according to how much detail you want to show on your finished piece of work. For instance, if you are working a big bold design and want to use a thick wool, then you should choose a wide mesh rug canvas, probably with three or five threads to the inch (2.5cm). On the other hand, if you decide to work a miniature of your house, then you should choose a small mesh canvas, possibly with 18 threads to the inch (2.5cm), and work the design in stranded cottons or two threads of crewel wool. A good all-round canvas for general work is a 13 or 14 thread to the inch (2.5cm) grade, used with three strands of crewel wool or two of Persian yarn.

Having chosen the size of mesh, the next choice is between interlock and interwoven types of canvas. In the manufacture of interlock canvas the vertical threads divide round the horizontal threads and lock them into place, ensuring that the canvas does not fray and the square meshes keep their shape. So long as interlock canvas is of good quality, that is without knots and of reasonable weight, it is a good choice as it is easy for a beginner to work with, and is especially suitable if you are not using a frame to keep the canvas taut. Interwoven canvas, as its name implies, is woven in a similar way to a fabric, and again there are different qualities, the best relying on superior polished cotton yarns for their stiffness, rather than excessive sizing. If used without a frame, the threads may begin to slip about when the canvas has been handled a lot, and the squares will become mis-shapen. This makes it impossible to keep the stitchery even. It is therefore always best to use a frame with interwoven canvas. Usually interwoven canvases are available in different colours, white, ecru and brown, but interlock canvas is invariably white. Any canvas may be coloured slightly with dryish acrylic paints, coloured pencils or waterproof fibre-tipped pens if a large number of straight stitches are being used, which may not fully cover the canvas.

Threads: There is no hard and fast rule as to what sorts of threads may or may not be used in needlepoint, but for general work the choice is usually a crewel wool or Persian yarn, and for miniature work six-stranded embroidery cottons such as Madeira embroidery floss or crewel wools. Tapestry wools may also be used but are restricted to a canvas of ten threads to the inch (2.5cm) as they cannot be divided. They also tend to get rather furry if handled a great deal and, of course, no shading within the needle is possible.

Crewel wools have the great advantage of being very fine, which means that when working on a 13s or 14s mesh canvas and using three strands of wool, there is the possibility of varying the shades of wool in the needle quite considerably, thus adding interest to the finished work, especially pictures. Crewel wools may just as easily be used on wide-mesh canvases although a great deal of wool is required, so usually special rug wools are chosen.

Another thread which may satisfactorily be used is Persian yarn which is made up of three 2-ply strands loosely plied together. These, though not quite as versatile as the crewel wools, are nevertheless high quality products, good to use if you do not want to mix the colours in the needle very much.

Cotton perle threads, which are tightly plied and shiny, may be used on their own or as highlights among other materials such as wool.

Soft cotton embroidery thread may also be used and its rather string-like texture is good for pictures worked entirely in satin stitch.

All these threads have very comprehensive colour ranges.

Needles: Always use tapestry needles and choose the correct size for the canvas you are working with. The correct size needle will not fall through the holes, neither will it distort the edges of the hole unduly when pulled through. The correct size for 18s canvas is 22, and for 12s, 13s and 14s it is 20.

Frames: Many different types of needlepoint frame are now available, some made to be held in the hand while others are floor-standing models. Make sure you choose one which is wide enough for the canvases you are likely to use, but no wider as frames can become unwieldy, though having said that, the wider ones sometimes rest easily across the arms of a chair. It should always be possible to roll the length of the canvas round the top and bottom of the frame, then tighten the bars sufficiently to hold the exposed canvas quite taut for working. The sides of the canvas may be laced to the frame.

Other necessary items: These include a large pair of scissors for cutting the canvas and a small pair with pointed ends for using as you work. An HB pencil or pale-coloured permanent fibre-tipped pen is useful for putting your designs on the canvas, plus materials for the finishing process which are mentioned in that section.

TECHNIQUES

Thread length: The length of the working thread should not be longer than about twenty inches (50cms) because the continual backwards and forwards movement through the canvas wears the thread gradually until it is much thinner than it was originally. If you are working a very small stitch it is advisable to use a shorter length.

Threading the needle: This can present problems. One answer is to use a threading tool available from needlework shops. Otherwise fold the end of the thread over the eye end of your needle and holding it tightly between thumb and first finger, extract the needle. Push the eye of the needle gently on to the resulting small fold and pull the thread through the eye.

Starting and finishing a length of thread: If you are starting off a new piece of thread on a bare part of the canvas, a good method is to hold about three quarters of an inch (2cm) of thread on the back of the work and sew over it until it is firmly held down, and then cut off the end flush with the back of the work. Do not leave any loose ends which may get pulled through to the front with another stitch. Once you have some stitchery on your canvas, you can start the next piece of thread by pulling it through the existing backing for half to three-quarters of an inch (1-2cm). Finish off your thread in the same way .

Stitches and stitching: Your stitches should be worked firmly to produce an even tension, otherwise the finished work cannot look smart. You should use stab stitch, that is, the needle and thread should be taken right through to the back or front of the work each stitch before being inserted again for the start of the next stitch. This facilitates an even tension and results in less wear on the thread.

Compensation stitches: This is the name given to those parts of stitches which you have to make when a whole stitch will not fit in the space you have left. Usually it is possible to work part of the main stitch and then fill the rest of the space with smaller stitches running in the same direction. Occasionally with a stitch such as Oriental it is not obvious how the compensation stitches at the beginning of the row should be placed. In such a case it is best to place one of the whole stitches in relation to the preceding row and then go back to insert the compensation stitches.

FINISHING

How you finish off your work after all the stitching is done is of vital importance, as invariably there is some distortion of the canvas by the stitchery, and even if everything looks neat and the right shape, a good stretching will still work wonders.

Materials:

1. A piece of board (plywood, chipboard, fibreboard) larger than your piece of canvas, marked out with lines at right angles to help to align your work. Cover the board with transparent plastic if any colour is likely to come off on to your work.
2. Staple gun or 3/4 inch (1.5cm) tacks.
3. LAP (or other starch) paste, available from hardware stores.
4. Piece of towelling the size of your work if you have used three-dimensional stitches.
5. Round-ended kitchen knife.
6. Cloth for dampening stitchery.

Method:

If possible, mark out on your board the exact size the work should be, so that you can pull the stitched area to these lines.

Dampen the back of the stitched area only with a damp cloth, especially if the canvas is very mis-shapen.

Place a piece of towelling the size of the stitched area on the board if you have used three-dimensional stitches and place the worked canvas, face down, over it.

Starting with one side of the work, line up the edge of the stitched area with one side of the marked area on the board and fasten down about 1/2 inch (1cm) away from the work with staples or tacks approximately 1/2 inch (1cm) apart. Work round the other three sides, pulling hard to get the canvas straight, flat, and the correct size, dampening again if necessary.

When you are happy with the size and shape, mix a little LAP paste to a light and fluffy consistency with water. With the knife work the paste into the back of the work, not too fiercely, but enough to penetrate into the fibres to some extent. Do not leave a lot of excess paste on the back of the work, and apply only a little paste to areas without much thread on the back. Leave to dry naturally in a warm place.

Some people do not trust the use of the paste, though the author has had no trouble with this method over many years. If you prefer not to use paste, be prepared to stretch your canvas again if it pulls back out of shape after the first attempt.

Choosing a Design

HELPFUL HINTS

Designing is a big subject which can only be touched on here, but perhaps a few hints may get you started.

Do not be frightened by the idea of designing your own canvases, nor feel that you are cheating if you use as the basis for your idea a favourite postcard, photograph or picture. By the time you have chosen your own colours and translated the whole thing into stitchery, there will not be much left of your original. Pictures are easier subjects to design for canvas than regular patterns, as the exact placing of the elements is not critical.

A photocopier, particularly if it enlarges and reduces, is a great help at the design stage, especially for pictorial subjects. For instance, a small picture of a house may be enlarged to the size required and this immediately gives you the correct positioning and size of the windows and other vital measurements.

One of the difficulties encountered when using a realistic picture as inspiration for needlepoint is that the original includes a great deal of detail which must be discarded for the medium of stitchery. Half-close your eyes to see which are the vital design elements and what may safely be left out or merely suggested. Extra detail may be added later as surface stitchery.

Draw, trace or photocopy your design on to paper, go over the outlines with a dark felt tip, and then if you are using a white canvas, it is very easy to place this over the design and trace it off using an HB pencil or a permanent, pale-coloured, fibre-tipped pen. Do not use a dark-coloured pen or pencil as this will show through any pale threads you may use.

If you want to include a variety of interesting stitches in your design, do not make the area for each one too small. Most of the stitches included in this book only look their best after several rows. When choosing stitches to use, try to put next to one another those which run in different directions and have different textures. In landscapes it is a good idea to select stitches which emphasise the subject, such as leaf stitches for trees and a diagonal stitch for a hillside. Do not feel you have to know exactly which stitch you are going to use in every area before you start, as it is usually much easier to decide what will look best when there is stitchery already on the canvas to give you ideas.

When you have got your design on to the canvas, do not spend time staring at the blank mesh. Make a start on the stitching, even if you take it all out later.

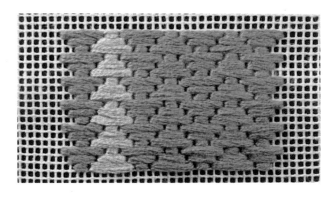

Arrowhead stitch is worked horizontally over 2, 4, 6 threads of the canvas and then repeated. The longest stitch of the second row abuts the shortest stitch of the first row.

Worked in one colour a wavy pattern is produced, whereas if two colours are used, alternating the colour each row, an interesting striped pattern emerges.

This is a quick background stitch which can also be used for sky in a landscape, or as a component of a patterned design.

Arrowhead is a good stitch for covering large areas as it does not distort the canvas.

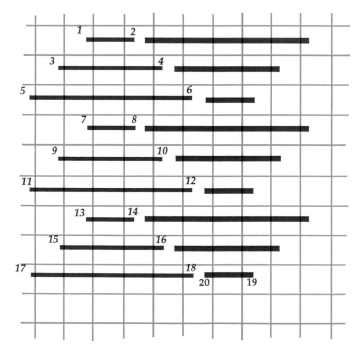

Back stitch is extremely useful in needlepoint as it may be used to outline irregularly shaped features which the square mesh of the canvas would otherwise make difficult to define accurately. This versatility is due to the fact that back stitches may vary in length to follow the line required. When an outline has been stitched, the inside of the feature can be filled with any stitch required.

Back stitch may also be used to fill in when some bare canvas has been left between other stitches.

Follow the numbering carefully, noticing that the stitches are indeed worked backwards. Back stitches are usually worked over two threads of canvas, but may be varied according to need.

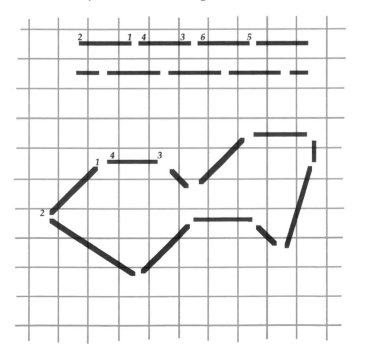

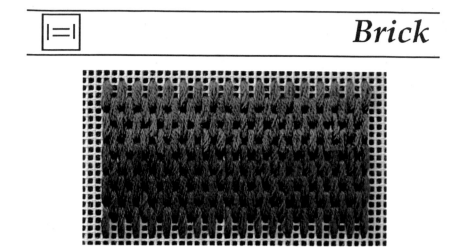

Basic brick stitch is worked vertically over four canvas threads. Several rows are needed to achieve the best effect. The tops of the second row stitches are worked into the middle holes between the stitches of the first row. It is easiest to add the compensation stitches after the second row has been worked.

Brick stitch may also be worked sideways to give a contrasting effect, and different coloured rows give interesting variations.

As with all straight stitches, brick stitch does not distort the canvas but may not always cover well, so be prepared to add more strands of thread in the needle if necessary.

Neat in appearance and quick to work, brick stitch is equally useful for patterned or pictorial designs, backgrounds or main subjects.

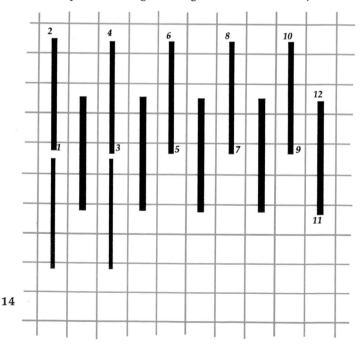

14

This miniature of a country church was worked by the author on 18s interlock canvas using Madeira six-strand embroidery floss. The greens chosen were dark and muted colours to fit in with the evening sky.

The stitches used include Florentine in different shades and mixtures of blue, pink, yellow and peach for the sky, single cross and French knots for the trees, single brick stitch worked sideways for the church, diagonal ground and single trammed Gobelin for the churchyard, French knots for the sheep and also for the gravel path, though the knots in the path were worked using only three strands of embroidery floss so that they would be smaller.

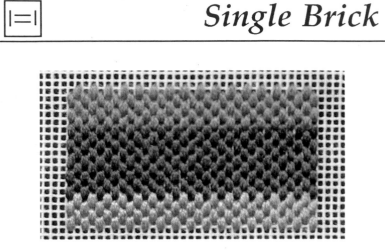
This is a half size version of brick stitch and is worked in exactly the same way, though the finished effect is quite different.

The second row is worked into the hole left between the stitches of the first row, and the compensation stitches cover just one thread of canvas.

Single brick stitch is very useful for small pieces of work, especially for architectural features such as roofs and doors. It also makes a neat background stitch as an alternative to tent.

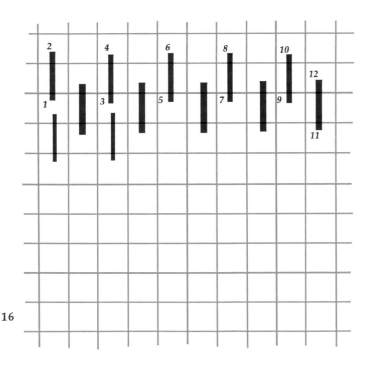

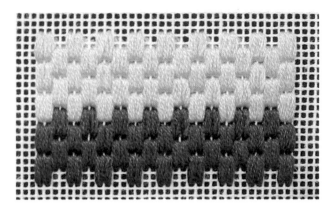

Double brick is worked in exactly the same way as brick stitch except for the fact that pairs of upright stitches are worked instead of singles. Make quite sure that you leave two holes between each pair of threads for the stitches of the second row.

This stitch gives a much chunkier effect than brick stitch and may be used successfully for tiles on a roof or stitched sideways as a wall. As a background stitch it is very quick to work.

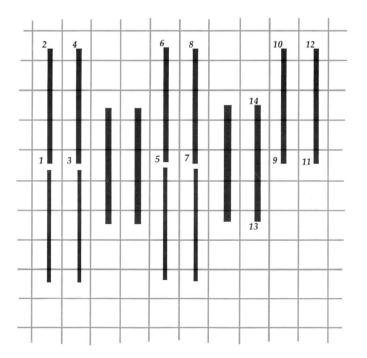

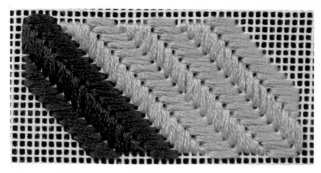

Chevron is a straight stitch which has the appearance of a diagonal stitch. It is very easy to work, but the compensation stitches must be carefully worked out. As with other straight stitches chevron sometimes does not cover the canvas well, so be prepared to add another strand of thread in the needle if necessary.

The stitch is worked in two parts, firstly a line of horizontal straight stitches is worked down a diagonal over three or four canvas threads, then a line of vertical straight stitches of the same length is worked into the ends of the stitches on the first row.

There are opportunities in this stitch for shading of colours or use of two colours. Even with the same colour the light catches the horizontal and vertical threads differently, thus giving the appearance of two shades.

Chevron can be used very effectively in pictures as a sloping hillside or varied colour sky, and being straight does not distort the canvas.

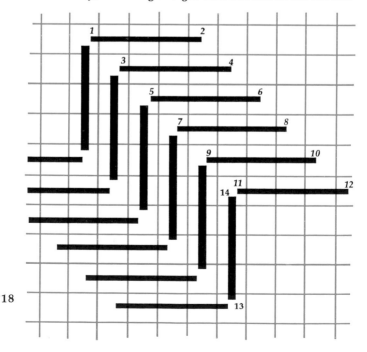

18

Diamond Straight

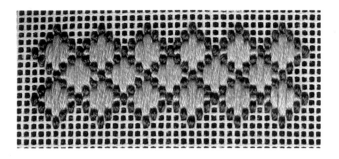

The diamonds show up best if two colours are used for this formal but pretty stitch. The diamond motif is made up of five upright stitches over 1,3,5,3,1 horizontal canvas threads. A gap of one hole (two threads) is left before the start of the next motif.

When a line of motifs has been worked, small stitches over one horizontal canvas thread are worked round each diamond, thus forming diamond shapes themselves.

Diamond straight in two colours would be a very suitable all-over stitch for an article such as a stool top. With its formal outlines it is not used much in pictorial work.

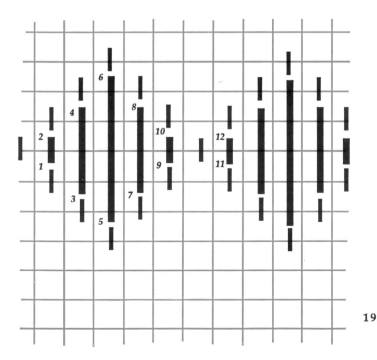

Florentine stitches are varying patterns of parallel vertical stitches. Usually these are worked in regular ups and downs, and fantastic effects can be achieved with clever use of colour and the arrangement of different length stitches.

To obtain the best results the tension must be very even. The parallel stitches catch the light and contrast well with other stitches. Do not be tempted to save wool by cutting the corners instead of working 'over and over'. The stitches will not lie flat if worked in this way.

Florentine stitches may also be worked randomly without regular patterns, and in pictures these would simulate such features as rock formations, flames or sunset effects.

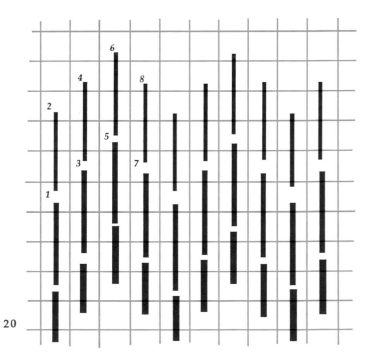

20

Hungarian makes a very neat stitch which gives the effect of diagonal lines of diamonds when used over a large area. It is very easy to work once you realise that a gap of two threads (one hole) must be left between each motif of three upright stitches.

This stitch is very effective when used for pictorial areas which need to look smooth yet require some interest — fields in the background of a landscape, interior walls, lawns — all look good in Hungarian stitch. On a patterned design it makes a foil for more dramatic stitches.

The stitch is worked over 2,4,2 horizontal canvas threads, then a gap of two threads is left before repeating the motif. The second row is worked back from right to left, with the long stitch being worked into the gap between the motifs of the first row. Notice that all the short stitches come under each other, as do the long stitches. Rows may be worked in different colours to give a striped effect.

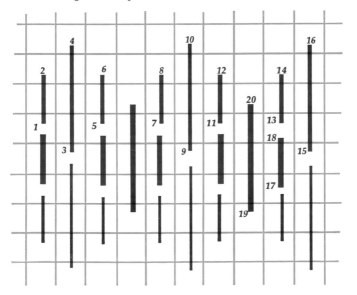

=│ *Hungarian Diamonds*

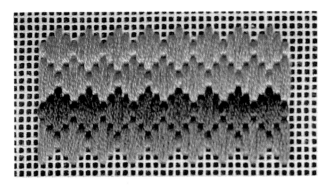

Hungarian diamonds is one of the easiest and most effective stitches in needlepoint. A straight stitch, it may be worked vertically or horizontally, but may need extra thread in the needle to cover really well.

Upright stitches are worked over 2,4,6,4 canvas threads and then repeated. The second row is worked back from the end of the first, the long stitches fitting up against the short stitches of the row above.

This stitch makes a bold foreground in landscapes, while it can easily be fitted into any shape on a patterned design. If a row of a particular length is to be worked, the stitch may be started in the middle of the row and worked out to either end to ensure that the diamonds are symmetrical. Single diamonds may be used as motifs.

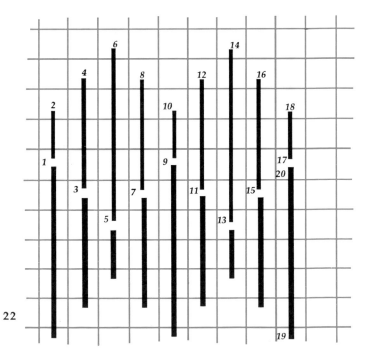

In this stitch the small Hungarian motif (lilac) worked over 2,4,2 canvas threads is placed two threads apart between rows of Florentine satin stitch (turquoise). The middle stitch of the motif may be worked in two parts as on the photograph.

In this particular Hungarian grounding the Florentine stitches are worked over four threads of canvas and rise or fall one thread each stitch. Many other variations are possible on the same theme. The Hungarian motif may be worked in a different colour as on the sample, which results in a striking pattern, or in the same colour.

This is not a suitable stitch for a pictorial subject, but can look very dramatic in a patterned piece of work.

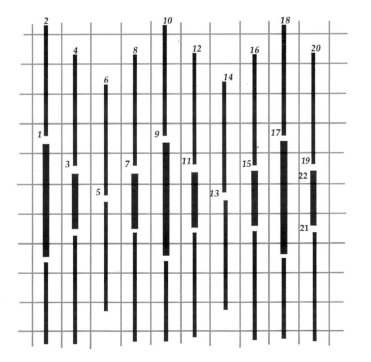

23

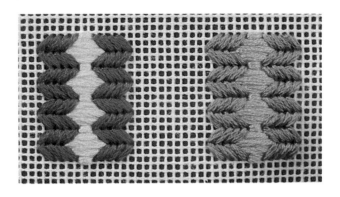

Indian stripe is made up of a vertical line of Hungarian diamonds bounded on either side by a herringbone design in diagonal stitches.

First stitch the diamonds over 2,4,6,4 vertical canvas threads, repeating as many times as required. Next add the diagonal stitches following the positioning and numbering on the diagram.

Indian stripe may also be stitched horizontally and is useful as a component in patterned designs or as a border.

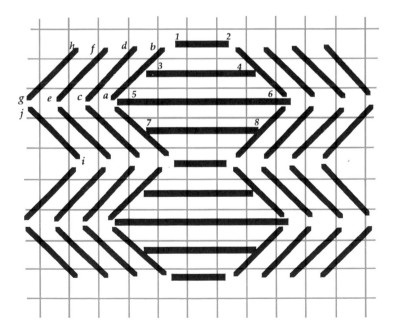

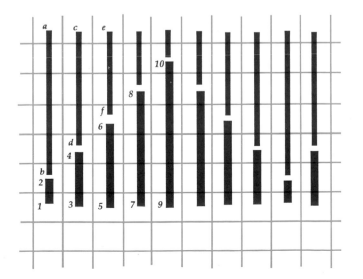

Long stitch is very useful in patterned designs, but is not suitable for landscape subjects. Different colour combinations can be used to achieve special effects. Extra thread may be needed in the needle to cover the canvas completely.

Upright stitches are worked over 1,2,3,4,5,4,3,2 horizontal canvas threads and then the sequence is repeated as many times as necessary. Next, from above this line of stitchery, other straight stitches, possibly in a different colour, are worked over 5,4,3,2,1,2,3,4 canvas threads down into the same holes as the tops of the first stitches. You must work 'over and over', and not try to save thread by cutting across the top. If you do this the stitches will not lie straight.

Care must be taken when starting the second row to begin high enough to fit the shortest stitches above the longest stitches of the first row — leave five bare threads above the shortest stitch of the first row.

If working long stitch along the side of say a needlecase, and wanting one of the long stitches in the middle of the row, it is easiest to start in the middle and work outwards in both directions.

25

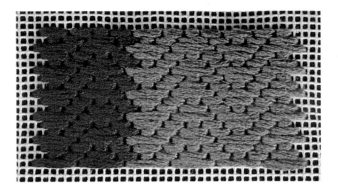

Straight Oriental is a bold, flowing stitch which like its diagonal counterpart needs to cover a large area to be seen at its best. It has the advantage over diagonal Oriental in that it will not distort the canvas.

Arrowheads are stitched over 2,4,6 vertical canvas threads, then stitches over three canvas threads are placed up against the two shorter stitches of the arrowhead.

The next row of arrowheads faces in the opposite direction, with the longest parts of the stitches (over six threads) abutting each other.

Straight Oriental can be successfully used as a background stitch, as a component in a patterned piece of work or as a sea or sky in a picture. This stitch may also be worked sideways.

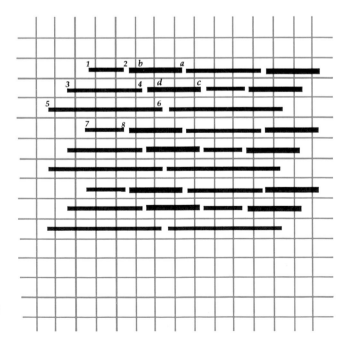

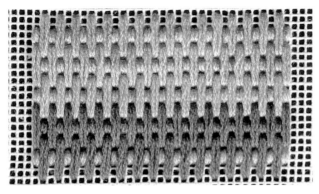

Parisian is a favourite stitch which, in common with all straight stitches, may be worked either vertically or horizontally. If the canvas shows through and this is not liked, it is possible to add an extra thread to those in the needle.

The large Parisian stitch is worked over six and two horizontal threads. Variety may be introduced by working the short stitches in a different colour or shade of the same colour.

Parisian is a neat stitch which can be used as a background or filling stitch or for large features such as architecture and hillsides on pictures.

Small Parisian is exactly the same as Parisian except that it is half the size, being worked over three and one horizontal threads. It is useful in miniature work.

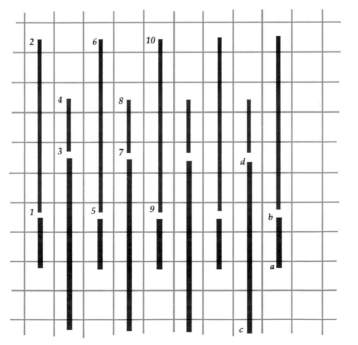

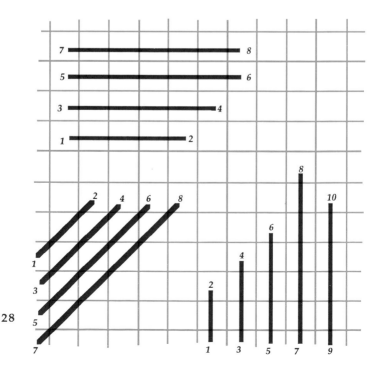
Satin stitches are any stitches which are laid down next to and parallel to each other, whether horizontally, vertically or diagonally, and as such are component parts of many other stitches such as Byzantine, Scottish and Hungarian diamonds.

With its smooth surface, satin stitch catches the light well, even when worked in wool, and by altering the direction of the stitches, interesting plays of dark and light areas may be obtained.

Whole pieces of work may be done in satin stitch, or it may be put into pictures and patterned pieces as a foil for more three-dimensional stitches and to highlight its own special qualities.

Satin stitch should always be worked in an 'over and over' fashion so that the stitches lie completely parallel.

Satin squares may be used singly as a central or corner motif, or may be placed next to each other to make up a background pattern.

Triangles of satin stitch are made at right angles to each other, starting in the centre over one canvas thread and working outwards until the square is as large as is required. If the stitch is being used as a background, the longest stitch on each side of the square is common to two squares.

Satin squares are rather too formal to be used in pictorial work, but are a very useful component of patterned pieces.

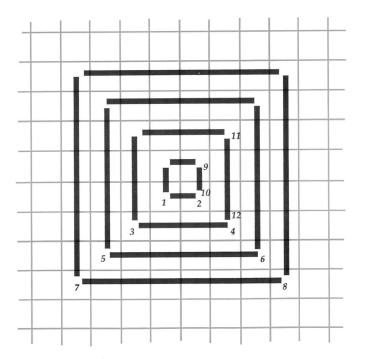

Single Trammed Gobelin

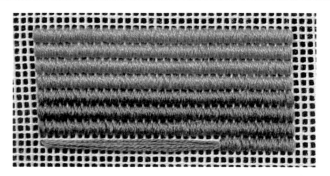

Single trammed Gobelin is a most useful three-dimensional stitch which has a pronounced ribbed effect. It may be worked either vertically or horizontally, depending on the effect required. It looks good as fields, roofs, fence posts or as a contrast to flat stitches in a patterned composition.

The tramming thread is laid down first, the entire length of the row required. It must neither buckle the canvas nor lie too loosely. The stitch is then worked vertically over the tramming thread and two horizontal canvas threads from the end of the tramming thread back to the beginning of the row. All subsequent rows should be worked in the same direction as otherwise the stitches will lie unevenly. The tramming thread for the second row is laid down two canvas threads down from the first and worked back to the beginning in the same manner.

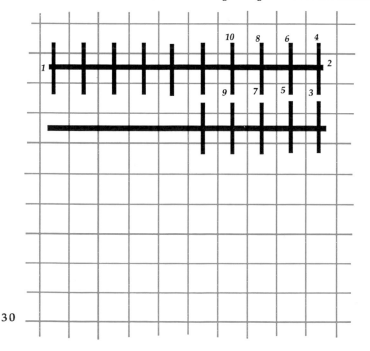

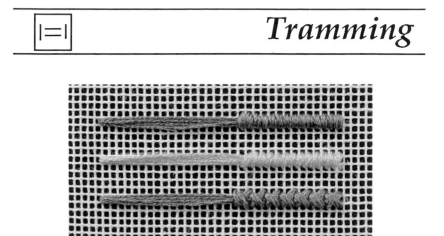

Tramming threads are never seen on a finished piece of needlepoint. They are threads laid down along the line the stitching is to take and the stitches are worked over them. Their purpose is either to strengthen the finished surface in such pieces as church kneelers which will receive a great deal of wear, or to give the stitchery a more three-dimensional quality, as in single trammed Gobelin stitch. Stitches which may be worked over a tramming thread include tent, cross and Gobelin.

On a double canvas the threads are laid down between the double threads, but on a single canvas they have to be laid down between the appropriate horizontal or vertical threads of canvas.

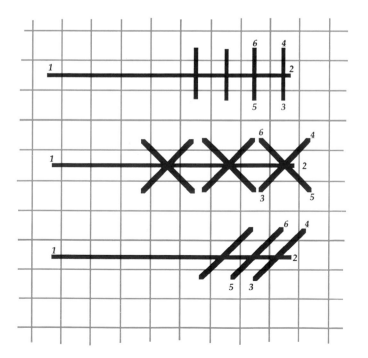

Triangle stitch consists of squares built up from four satin stitch triangles worked over 2,3,4,5,4,3,2 canvas threads. Cross stitches are worked at each corner to cover the canvas threads which would otherwise be bare. The triangles can be any size within reason and the crosses may be worked in a contrasting colour to vary the effect.

This is a stitch which is quickly worked and makes a good stool covering if the triangles are not made too large. Very long threads would catch rather easily.

Triangle stitch is not generally used in pictorial work.

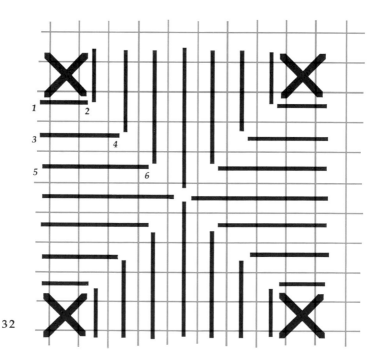

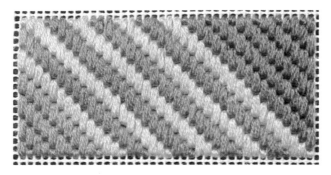

Twill is a versatile straight stitch which steps down the diagonals of the canvas, giving the appearance of diagonal stripes. This is very useful for large areas such as skies on pictures, where a true diagonal stitch such as diagonal ground would distort the canvas to some extent. Subtle shadings can be introduced by using different colours in the needle together, and changing the combination every so often.

Work vertical stitches over three or four horizontal canvas threads, stepping down one thread with each successive stitch. The next row can be worked up from the bottom, for although the back looks different, the stitches on the front of the work look even.

Double twill is worked in the same way, except that the alternate rows are over a smaller number of threads, either one or two, depending on the size of the first row stitches.

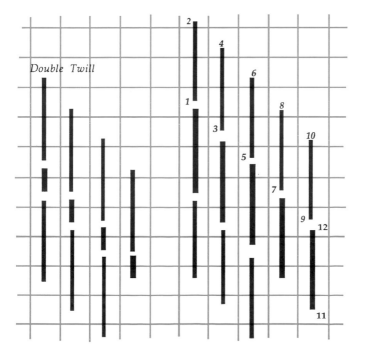

Double Twill

33

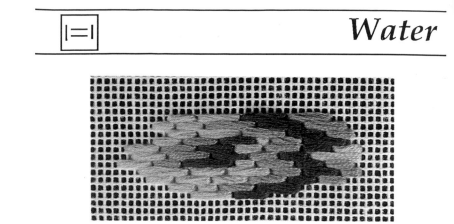

Water stitch is, in fact, a random long and short satin stitch worked in a particular way, but this method works so well for watery subjects that it deserves an entry of its own.

To achieve the correct effect, the long and short stitches should not be worked in and out along the rows as though darning (lower diagram), but should be zig-zagged up and down the area to be covered, in such a way that the thread on the reverse is always taken back towards the stitch just worked, so that the hole is left open for another stitch to be inserted without splitting the thread (upper diagram).

The back looks messy, but the finished effect on the front is worth it, particularly if you choose and mix your colours well to give patches of light and shade on the water.

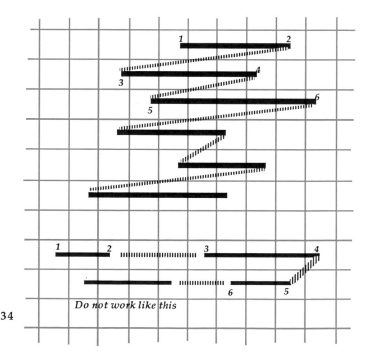

Do not work like this

Waterfall

As its name implies, this stitch can be used very satisfactorily to represent falling water, where a more regular stitch would not look realistic. Several different colours can be used to give a naturalistic effect, while the splitting of the stitches contributes towards the illusion of a continuous flow of water.

Although the stitchery looks completely random, obviously it is necessary to give some thought to where you want concentrations of the different colours to achieve the desired effect. With two colours in the needle, work straight, upright stitches over different numbers of horizontal canvas threads, some long, others of medium length. Gradually fill up the whole area, varying the colours and splitting some stitches by pushing the needle and thread through them, in other cases push the needle in between stitches already in position.

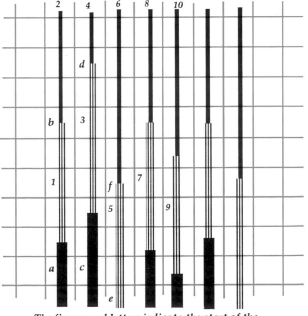

35

The figures and letters indicate the start of the stitch even if later hidden by a subsequent stitch

The Waterfall needlepoint was worked by the author on 5s
rug canvas, using ten strands of crewel wool in the needle.
Though extravagant, this gave excellent opportunities for
mixing wools in the needle. The original inspiration was a
piece of Tiffany stained glass. The actual size of the picture
is 29" x 18" (74 x 46cm).

Detail of right hillside.

Detail of waterfall, bank and foam.

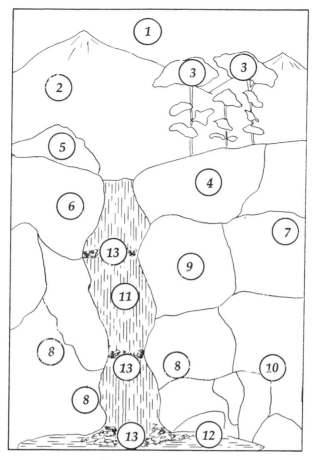

Key to numbering on chart.

1. Parisian stitch in various blues mixed in the needle.
2. Mountain stitch, white and various pale greys and blues
   mixed in the needle.
3. Single cross stitch, dark forest green.
4. Oblique Slav stitch, mixed greens.
5. French knots, mixed colours, simulating bushes.
6. Parisian stitch, mixed colours, some French knots on surface.
7. Wheel stitch motif, mixed orange and gold.
8. Octagonal eye, various mixed colours.
9. Crossed Gobelin, dark green and mixed green and blue.
10. Spider's web, gold and orange mixed.
11. Waterfall stitch, mixed turquoises and white.
12. Water stitch, various blues and white.
13. French knots and cut and uncut Turkish knots, making a very
    realistic spray.

Many other stitches, all included in this book.

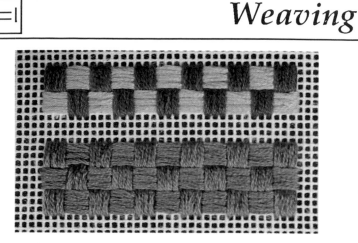

Weaving stitch is made up of groups of straight stitches at right angles to each other, giving the effect of an interwoven fabric. Worked in two colours chequerboard squares are produced.

Work three upright straight stitches over four horizontal canvas threads. Next bring the working thread out four canvas threads to the right of this group in the position shown on the diagram. Work three horizontal stitches into the holes just masked by the last upright thread, taking care not to split the threads. The next group of upright stitches is worked over the ends of the horizontal stitches. If working in two colours, use two needles rather than attempt to fill in afterwards. The second row is worked back from right to left.

Weaving stitch may be used in patterned pieces in square or.rectangular areas and in pictorial pieces for suitable subject matter such as baskets and mats.

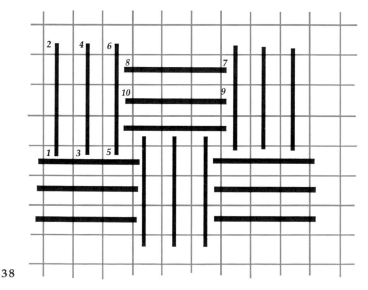

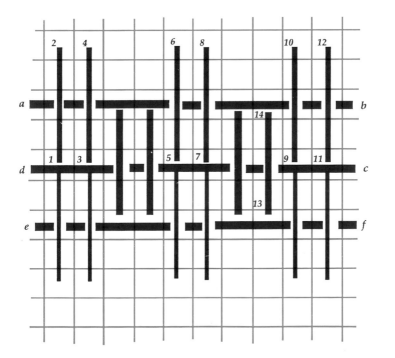

Willow is a variation of double brick stitch, although it looks completely different, especially if worked in two colours.

Work an area in double brick stitch and then take a contrasting coloured thread, which may be twisted to form a cord, and having brought it to the front of the work, thread it across the stitching as a surface stitch, behind the middle of the upright threads of the first row and across the top of row two. Follow this pattern in succeeding rows as shown on the diagram.

Willow is a formal stitch, more useful in patterned work than in pictures, though in appropriate colours it could represent tiling very well.

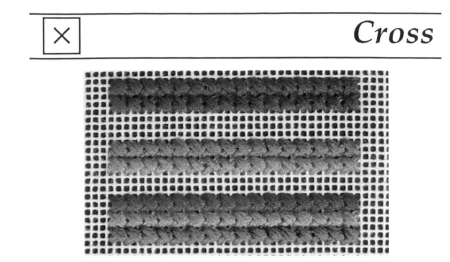

Cross is made up of two diagonal stitches each worked over two canvas intersections, the first being made from bottom left to top right and the second from bottom right to top left. The upper stitch of the cross is thus always made in the same direction.

Occasionally, to achieve a different and less homogeneous effect, the upper stitches may be alternated in direction, in which case in these alternate crosses the sequence of working the stitch is reversed.

This is one of the oldest needlepoint stitches and many pieces of work still use only this one stitch.

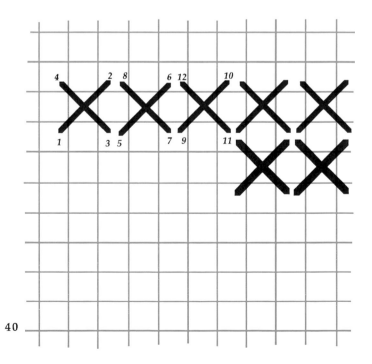

Single Cross

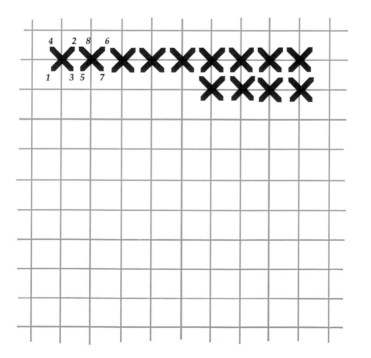

The cross formation is difficult to see in single cross stitch, in which a diagonal stitch is worked over just one canvas intersection in each direction. All the top stitches of the crosses should lie the same way.

The knobbly surface produced looks very good as fir trees on pictures.

Single cross is difficult to work over large areas as the stitches are so densely packed together, but if a really tough finish is required this stitch is incredibly hard wearing.

Single cross stitch was much used in the past where today tent stitch would probably be substituted, and at first glance it is difficult to tell the difference.

Double cross is worked over a square of either two or four threads of the canvas. Firstly an upright cross is stitched over two or four horizontal and two or four vertical canvas threads. A diagonal cross is then worked on top of it over the same number of threads in each direction.

Always make sure the diagonal cross is on top, otherwise this stitch becomes Smyrna cross. Also ensure that the top diagonal thread goes in the same direction on each cross.

Having the diagonal cross on top makes this a less firm stitch than Smyrna cross, and it is inadvisable to use the large double cross in situations where the stitching is to receive a lot of wear.

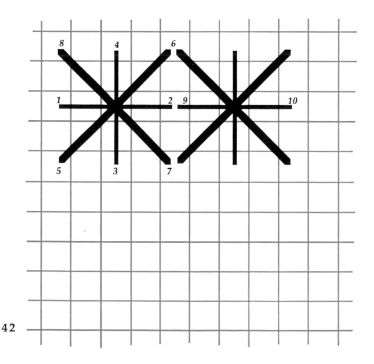

Smyrna Cross

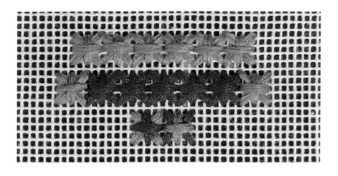

Smyrna cross is worked over two or four canvas threads. A diagonal cross is worked first and then a straight cross is stitched on top of it. Make sure that the same stitch of the straight cross is on top in each Smyrna cross.

With the straight cross on top, Smyrna makes a stronger stitch than double cross, but otherwise has a similar sculptured appearance which can be used to contrast with flatter stitches in any piece of needlepoint.

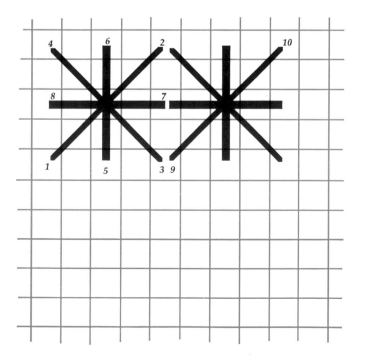

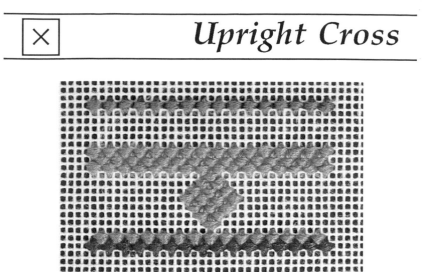

Upright cross forms a very neat and firm surface. It is worked over two vertical and two horizontal canvas threads. The tops of the uprights of the crosses on the second row go into the same holes as the cross bars of the row above.

A two-colour design can be worked on a patterned piece of stitchery, and various shapes may be made to represent trees, bushes and other features in pictures.

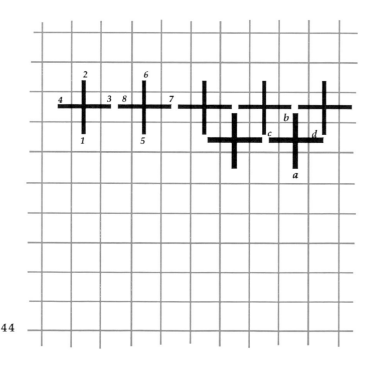

Fern is a very easy stitch which is worked in rows down the area to be covered. It is worked into every other hole, or every hole for a really close, thick cover. Each part of the stitch is worked over four horizontal and three vertical canvas threads. No bare threads are left between the rows.

Fern stitch makes a good figured background or shaded sky on a picture where the colour may be graduated through the different rows. For a sky the stitch may also be worked sideways by turning the canvas through ninety degrees.

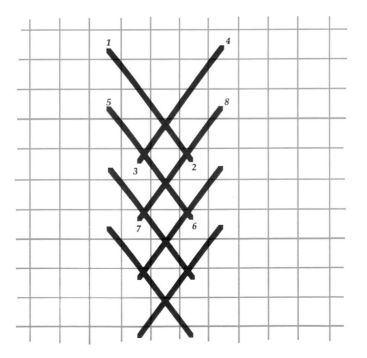

Crossed Gobelin is quick and easy to work and makes a firm and three-dimensional stitch which is useful as a large filling stitch or for making a textured feature on a picture.

A long vertical stitch over six canvas threads is made, and a cross stitch covering two threads in each direction is made over the centre of this upright, as shown on the diagram. The next vertical stitch is placed two canvas threads to the right to leave room for the cross.

The second row is worked back from right to left, a firm cover being achieved by the tops of the long stitches of the second row being worked into the holes where the crosses of the first row meet.

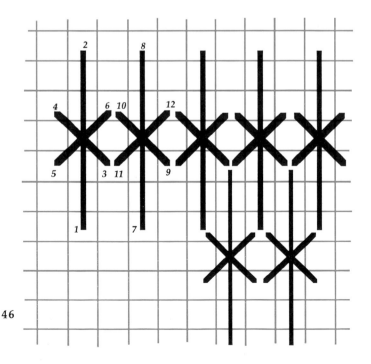

Double Leviathan

Double leviathan is worked over four threads in each direction and is actually a succession of different crosses on top of one another, so that in the end, every hole around the square is filled. It may be worked with either the straight or the corner-to-corner cross on top.

Care must be taken when working several double leviathan stitches together to work all the same crosses on top, unless a different regular pattern has been decided upon.

This makes an extremely high, hard stitch and is most useful in patterned work as a contrast to flatter stitches. As it is worked over four threads it can only be satisfactorily fitted into spaces in which the canvas threads are divisible by four.

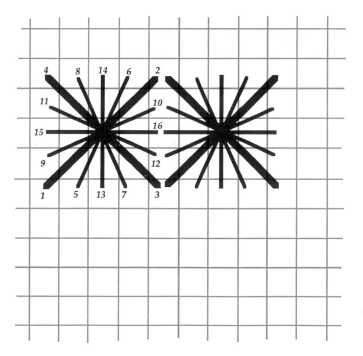

Long Legged Cross

Long legged cross is a plait-like stitch which makes a good edging on items such as needlecases, spectacles cases and cushions, because it is very firm and backings can be sewn to it in making up pieces of work. Three rows of long legged cross make a realistic spine on a folded item and two rows can be used on a right-angle bend such as a kneeler edge.

The stitch is usually worked across two horizontal canvas threads. If a flat end is required at the start of the row, a cross stitch over two threads either way must be worked first.

The first part of the main stitch is made across two horizontal and four vertical canvas threads. The needle is then brought out two canvas threads below and taken back to the top row over two diagonals to the left. The stitch is repeated from two canvas threads below this point. The thread already in position may mask the correct hole slightly.

Long legged cross variation is a neat, cord-like stitch worked in a similar way to the main stitch, only over one horizontal thread instead of two and three vertical threads rather than four. It can be used very effectively as a frame around pictures or to edge designs let into cushion fronts. It looks especially good worked in perle or stranded cottons.

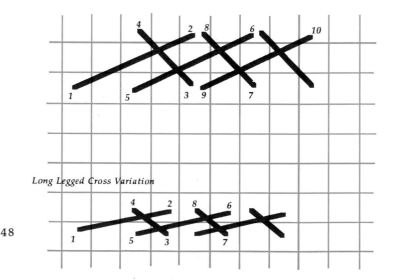

Long Legged Cross Variation

Norwich is a handsome, two-layer stitch which seems complicated to work until you grasp the logic of its construction. After the initial basic cross has been worked, all the following parts of the stitch are worked parallel to one or other of the arms of this cross, and when the needle has been brought to the front of the work, the hole to be used next is always down or along whichever side of the square you are already on, never across a corner. Follow the numbering carefully.

This stitch should be worked over an uneven number of canvas threads. If you need to work it over an even number of threads the last round of stitches will go into the middle hole on each side without crossing other threads.

Use a firm, smooth thread to show Norwich off to advantage. It may be used as a single motif or to cover a whole area in patterned work.

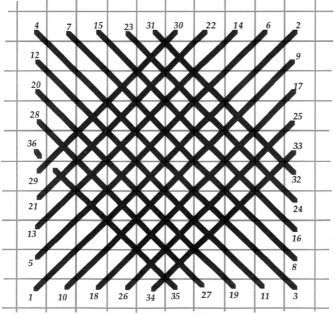

35/36 goes UNDER 29/30

49

Rhodes is a very thick, three-dimensional stitch which can be worked over a square of any number of threads, but needs to be quite large to show off to advantage. It may be used as a motif stitch and looks well in the corners of geometrical patterns. This is a stitch not much used in landscapes and as it stands up so high it tends not to wear very well.

Begin by working a diagonal stitch from corner to corner of the square selected. Moving to the right along the bottom and to the left along the top work diagonal stitches into every hole. When you come to the bottom right-hand corner start working up the right-hand side and down the left-hand side until every hole is filled. A small stitch may be made across the centre to hold the threads in place.

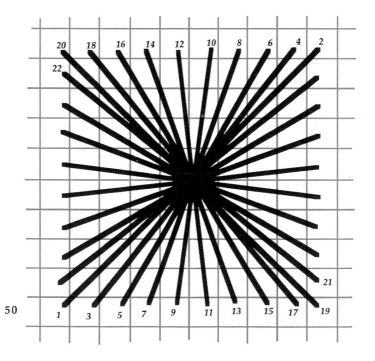

Patterned designs have to be carefully worked out before you start stitching, as otherwise you will find that the stitches you use do not fit in the spaces you have allowed for them. Many people find this mathematical planning very much to their liking, whereas to others it is tedious. You will know into which group you fall and can avoid pieces of this type if they do not appeal to you.

The stitches used in this particular piece, which was designed to be made into a box pincushion, are, from the centre:

Four leaf stitches forming a motif surrounded by tent stitch

Rice stitch

Double leviathan stitch

Straight stitch flowers

Tent stitch

Long stitch with Rhodes stitches in the corners

Tent stitch

Long legged cross stitch

Tent stitch

Cushion stitch

Tent stitch

Long legged cross stitch

Rice is a versatile single or two-colour stitch, mainly used in patterned pieces of work. The whole character of the stitch can be altered by using two colours instead of one, and then changed again by reversing the colours.

Begin by stitching a line of large cross stitches over a square of four canvas threads, making sure that all the top threads are worked in the same direction. Then, with the second colour if one is being used, work short stitches diagonally across each of the legs of the crosses from the middle hole between any pair of legs to the middle hole between the next adjacent pair.

When using rice stitch in a row of a defined length, make sure the number of canvas threads is divisible by four so that you do not have to end with part of a stitch.

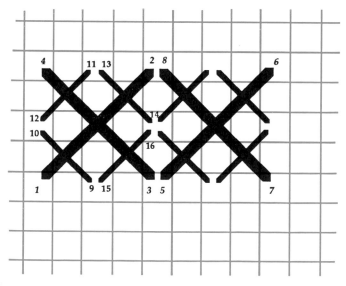

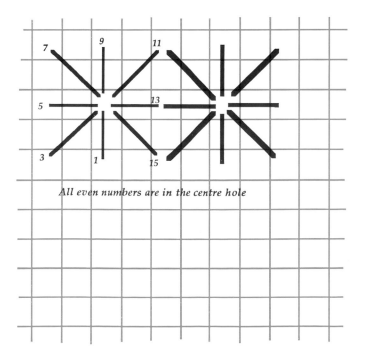

A simple eyelet stitch, in which eight stitches are worked over two diagonal and two straight canvas threads into the centre.

This stitch may be worked rather better on interwoven canvas where the threads can be easily moved apart to leave a central hole, than on interlock canvas, where the canvas threads are held in place. If using interlock canvas therefore, enlarge the centre hole with a large-diameter needle before starting.

Algerian eye does not cover the canvas well, but this can be a feature of the design. Back stitches in a different colour can be worked over two threads round each stitch if the canvas needs to be hidden.

Take care not to let any of the working threads show through the central hole on the front when moving from one stitch to the next.

All even numbers are in the centre hole

Diamond Eyelet

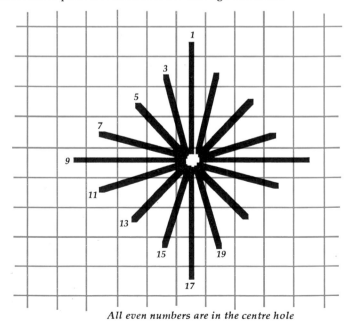

Diamond eyelet may be worked on either interlock canvas, where the threads are locked together, or interwoven, where they are not. In both cases the centre hole must first be carefully enlarged with a thick needle or stiletto. When using interlock canvas the hole must be fully enlarged before starting to sew as it is difficult to enlarge further later.

Having anchored the thread well, start off with a long stitch over four canvas threads from the top of the stitch into the centre hole. Follow the diagonal down one side of this stitch and work three other stitches into the centre until you reach the next long stitch at right angles to the first. Work round the eyelet in this manner, following the numbering. Pull the threads firmly to keep the centre hole open.

Eyelets grouped together may need a back stitch between to cover any exposed canvas. Eyelet stitches are very effective if a piece of contrasting material is placed behind to show through the holes.

All even numbers are in the centre hole

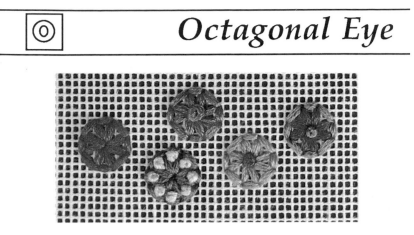

Octagonal eye has the appearance of a wheel with eight spokes. The spokes are worked into the centre as shown on the numbered diagram, and the ends of the spokes are then joined by back stitches. The centre hole may be enlarged before beginning with a blunt needle or the ends of small scissors. French knots of the same or a different colour may be placed in the centre and between the spokes.

This is a striking eyelet stitch which may be used to represent different features on a picture or as a motif in a patterned piece of work. A number of octagonal eyes may be joined up to make a background, in this case the diagonal back stitches become common to two eyes, and extra back stitches have to be added to cover bare canvas threads between the straight back stitches already in place.

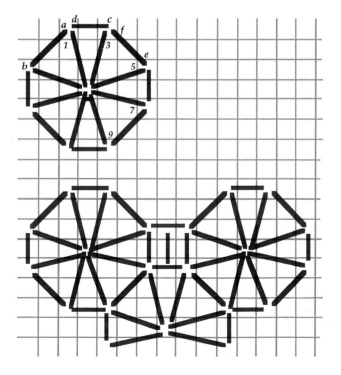

55

This small rug was worked by the author to fit over a stool. It has a large central motif adapted from a Persian carpet. It is worked on 5s rug canvas entirely in Turkish knots with ten strands of crewel wool in the special rug needle. The needle for this work is flat with a flat end which is slightly turned up to facilitate making the stitches.

Although it was very extravagant to work this rug in the fine crewel wools, the end result is so attractive and soft that the expense is soon forgotten. Obviously if you are working a rug for actually putting on the floor, then you would have to use sturdier thread, but it would then be difficult to achieve the close, fine pile of this rug.

Turkish Knot (Ghiordes Knot)

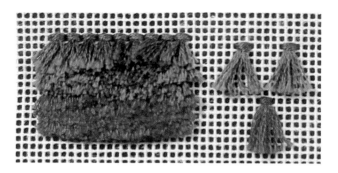

This is a pile stitch in which the pile stands upright when a few rows have been worked. Care must be taken when learning this stitch as it can be difficult to distinguish between the knot and the tuft. Work the rows from bottom to top.

1. Starting with the working thread on the front of the canvas take a stitch to the left behind one canvas thread. Pull until all the thread has been pulled through apart from that forming the length of the pile. Hold this down with your thumb.

2. With the loop of the thread towards the *top* of the work, take another stitch to the left behind the canvas thread next on the right, working into the same hole as before. Pull this tightly to form the knot.

3. Hold the working thread down below the knot and hold down the length of the pile while working the next stitch (you may form the pile round a knitting needle). Make sure that the working thread again lies to the *top* of the work while working the second half of the stitch.

4. Cut the pile of each row against a gauge before proceeding to the next row. Leave two canvas threads before working the next row.

Use the Turkish knot for animal fur, foam on water, whole stool tops or just as a contrast to other textures.

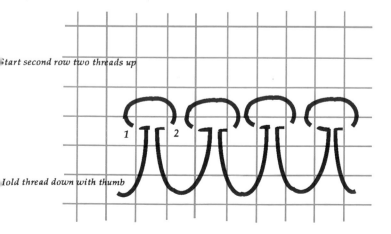

Start second row two threads up

Hold thread down with thumb

57

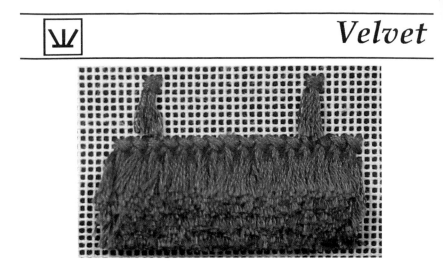
Velvet is a pile stitch which can be used as an alternative to the Turkish knot. It is easy to work with a little practice as it is based on a cross stitch. Velvet stitch pile does not stand up as vertically as Turkish knot pile.

Start with a diagonal stitch to the right over two intersections of the canvas. Bring the needle up through the original hole again and down through the second hole used, as though to repeat the second stitch on top of the first. However, do not pull the thread right through the canvas but leave a loop for the pile. You may make the loop round a knitting needle if you prefer. Next bring the needle out two canvas threads below where the needle last entered the canvas and finish off the cross stitch, making sure the loop is being stitched down. Work the second and successive rows above the first, leaving one horizontal canvas thread between the rows. The pile may be cut and trimmed each row or left uncut.

Velvet stitch may be used to make a complete piece of work, such as a rug, or alternatively used as a contrast to other stitches. Small areas do not wear well.

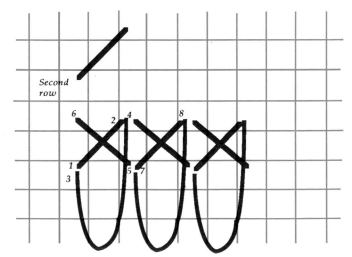

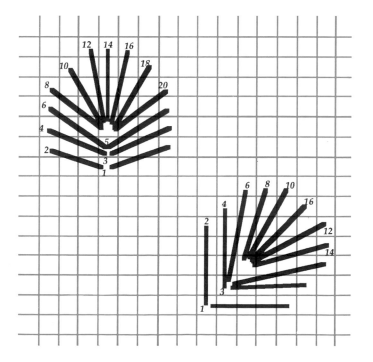

Chinese fan is a nicely rounded version of leaf stitch which looks very decorative as a frieze round a design, with diagonal Chinese fans in the corners. In a picture the fans make good bushes. A French knot may be inserted at the base of the fan, possibly in a second colour.

Follow the sequence of numbers, noting that the bottom hole is used only once for each side of the fan, the next hole is used twice each side, and the third hole is used seven times round the top.

In the diagonal version note that the first and second stitches on each side of the fan follow the vertical and horizontal lines of the canvas. There is one stitch each side from the first hole, two each side from the second hole, and five stitches round the top from the third hole. Note that the centre stitch of the five is put in last.

59

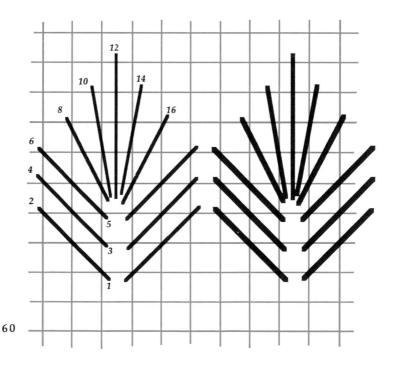

This is one of the most useful and popular stitches in needlepoint, being a basic stitch in both pictorial and patterned pieces of work. It can be used singly or combined with other leaf stitches to form motifs, French knots or stems may be added to create different effects, and its three-dimensional nature makes it stand out from a flatter background.

It must be worked carefully, following the sequence of numbers on the diagram. The three-dimensional effect is achieved by using the hole for the top part of the leaf five times.

Be sure to make the two sides of the leaf match — it is easy to make the right-hand side narrower by one thread, as when stitching in the correct holes the leaf looks rather too wide to begin with.

Leaf square is an effective but simply worked stitch which lends itself to wide variations of colour patterns. The leaf may be shaded from top to bottom in two or three shades of the same colour, or contrasting colours may be used. The stitch looks rather dull if worked all in the same colour. An extra variation is the back stitches which may be worked up the middle of the whole or part of the leaf.

Work from top to bottom of each leaf, both sides at once, that is, making stitches at right angles to each other, increasing in size by one thread each row. Follow the numbering on the diagram. The stitch may be varied considerably in size if required.

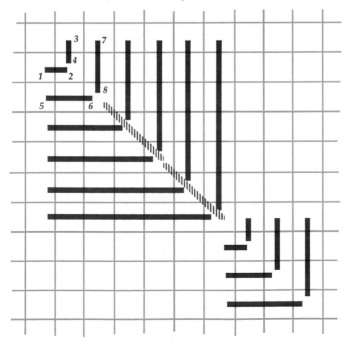

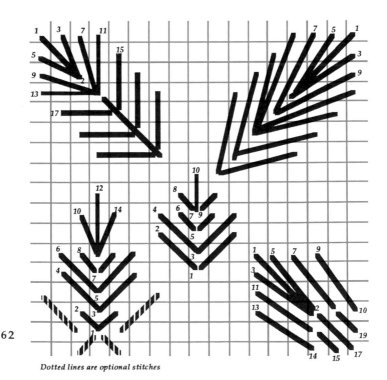

Diagrams are given here for various leaf stitches, differing in size and shape. It is useful to have a large number of such stitches to choose from so that pieces of work can be given variety and interest. Of course each diagonal leaf may be made to face either direction by reversing the direction of the stitches.

These leaves may also be varied by adding or subtracting parts of the stitch, and having seen how the motifs are put together you will be able to devise shapes of your own.

Dotted lines are optional stitches

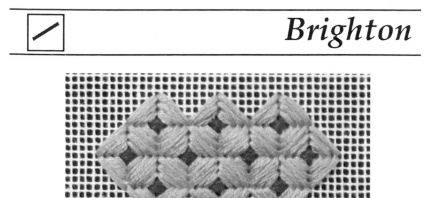

Brighton

This makes a very interesting and decorative large background stitch. Alternatively, one of the diamond shapes may be used as a single motif. The full effect of the stitch as a background is not seen until quite a large area has been worked.

Brighton stitch is worked outwards from one centre in four directions. Then from any one of the sides, stitches are worked reducing in size down to another centre. Again work outwards to build up the other three sides of the diamond. This may appear rather complicated, but by following the numbering carefully the pattern will soon emerge.

The centres are filled with upright crosses - possibly in another colour.

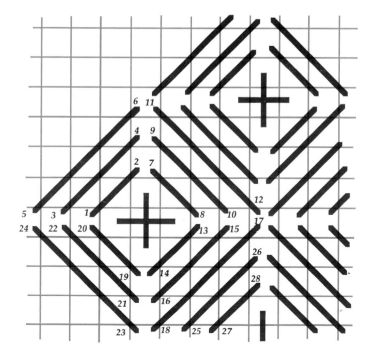

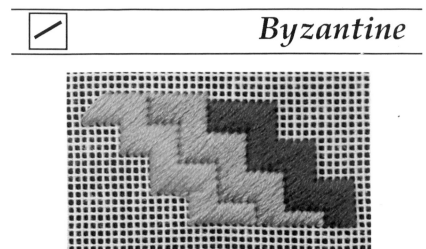

Byzantine is a bold, diagonal stitch which may distort the canvas if large areas are worked.

Parallel diagonal stitches are worked, usually over four canvas intersections, though this may be varied. The steps may be any width, but five or six stitches wide looks best. The thread must be pulled firmly but not tightly to make sure the threads lie evenly and flat, otherwise the smooth effect is lost.

Byzantine may be worked randomly with uneven sized steps, both in height and width. This can look very effective for paving and stonework.

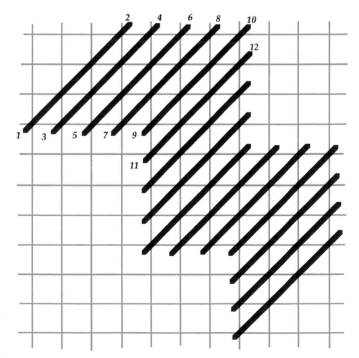

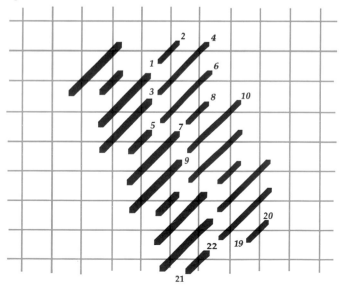

Cashmere is a very useful stitch which steps down the canvas at a steep angle, contrasting with other diagonally worked stitches. For this reason it is very useful in both pictures and patterned pieces.

Three diagonal stitches are placed under one another, the first being worked over one intersection of the canvas while the other two are each worked over two intersections. The short stitch of the next group is placed to the right of the second long stitch and the pattern continued as before.

The second row is worked from the bottom upwards, but be very careful about placing the first stitch as the pattern is not obvious. Note that the short stitches come one thread down and two threads to the left of those in the previous row and that the first long stitch is now placed to the left of the short. It may be found easiest to place a short stitch first as a guide.

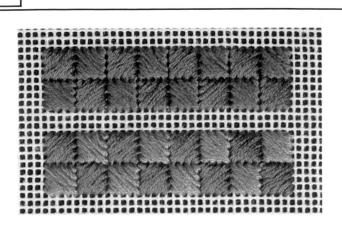

Cushion stitch is a particular variation of satin stitch in which squares are made up of groups of satin stitches facing two different ways. This is an effective and easily worked stitch, in which the light catching the differently worked threads makes them seem different colours.

The satin stitch squares are usually worked over 1,2,3,4,3,2,1 canvas intersections, firstly from left to right and then next to this group a similar square is worked with stitches worked from right to left. The squares are alternated on the second row to make a chequerboard pattern.

This is mainly a stitch for patterned designs and is little used in pictorial work, being too formal.

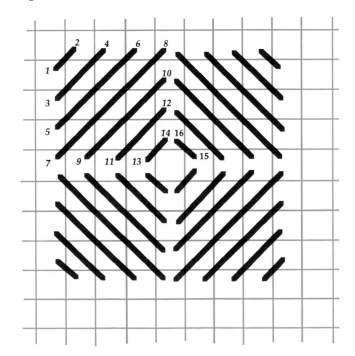

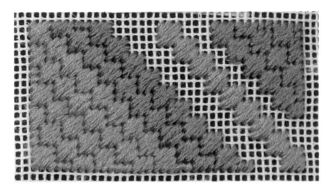

Diagonal ground is a most useful stitch and has the advantage of being very easy to work.

Diagonal stitches are made over 1,2,3,2 intersections of the canvas and the sequence is then repeated. On succeeding rows the longest stitch lies up against the shortest stitch of the previous row.

Subtle colour changes may be introduced if the stitch is used for a hillside in a picture by using different mixtures of colour in the needle for various parts of each row. If diagonal ground is used as a decorative stitch the rows may be worked in different colours or types of thread.

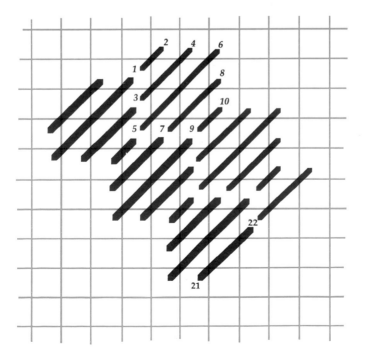

67

Many different stitches have been used in this shell picture which was originally drawn from life. The finished design has been mounted under strong transparent plastic to make a tray. The stitches include tent, brick, Hungarian, diagonal mosaic, French knots and Milanese. The finished shell was embellished with tiny black beads and French knots worked in silver thread.

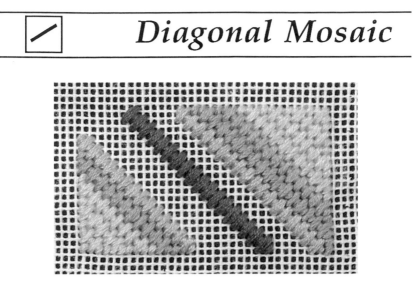

Diagonal mosaic is a simple diagonal stitch worked over 1,2 canvas intersections and then repeated. The long stitch of one row fits against the short stitch of the preceding row, the effect being quite ridged. If used as a sky on a landscape picture the rows can be varied in shade to create the effect of shafts of light.

As with all diagonal stitches, distortion of the canvas can occur if large areas are covered with this stitch.

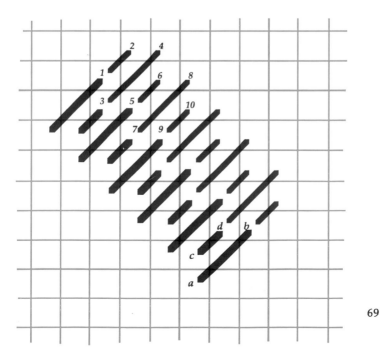

Fan is a simple stitch, radiating out usually from the bottom left-hand corner into every other hole round a square of four canvas threads. The fans may also be stitched from the bottom right-hand corner if required to face the opposite way, or the directions of the rows may be alternated. Although one or two fans do not seem to cover the canvas very well, when a whole section is stitched in either horizontal or vertical rows, the coverage is quite good.

With its slightly ragged edge, fan stitch makes a surprisingly realistic open type of tree in a pictorial piece of work, and may also be used effectively in one or more colours in patterned pieces.

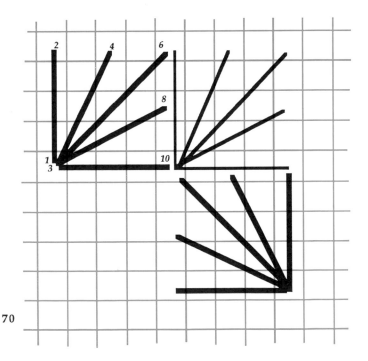

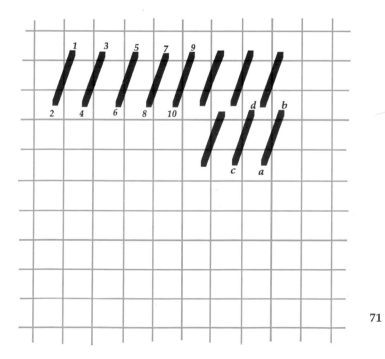

Gobelin

The Gobelin stitches are amongst the most traditional in needlepoint. This basic stitch is worked across one vertical and two horizontal canvas threads and appears neat and steeply diagonal.

The stitch is like an oversized tent stitch, and is worked in the same way to ensure a good covering of stitchery on the back, which will give strength. Gobelin may also be worked twice the height — over four horizontal threads.

Gobelin is useful for stripes and has a marked ribbed effect. In pictures it can be used for weatherboarding on houses.

Half Cross

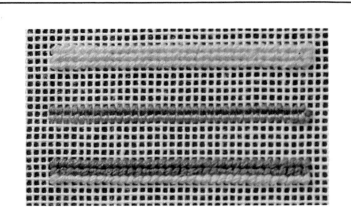

Half cross looks almost identical to tent stitch on the front of the canvas, but on the back is very different, with only small upright threads instead of a dense covering of diagonal stitchery. It is thus not such a strong stitch and is not recommended for any project which will need to wear well, such as a rug or stool top.

The great advantages of half cross stitch are that it does not distort the canvas as continental tent stitch does, and is economical in its use of thread. Each stitch is across one intersection of the canvas. Follow the numbering carefully, especially at the start of the second row.

If using half cross stitch make sure that every row has small vertical stitches on the back and not alternate rows of vertical and sloping stitches, which would indicate that by mistake you are doing every other row in tent stitch. On the picture above, the two middle rows show the *back* of the stitches. The canvas may be turned upside down to work the second and alternate rows if this is found to be easier.

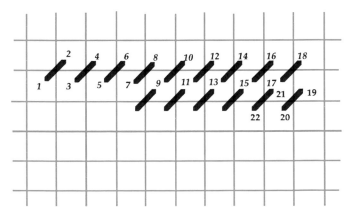

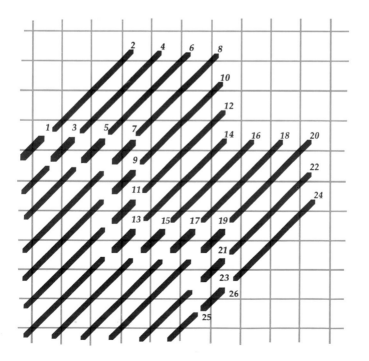

The first row making up this stitch consists of satin stitches over two or three canvas intersections worked in steps, usually of the same width. The second row is worked in tent stitch and looks very effective in a different colour or thread of a different texture.

Jacquard stitch may also be worked randomly with varied sizes of steps, as in the Tropical Rain Forest background (page 108). If worked over a large continuous area this stitch will distort the canvas.

By using a variety of similar colours within each row jacquard may be used very effectively for the sky of a picture, and the use of contrasting colours in patterned pieces looks very dramatic.

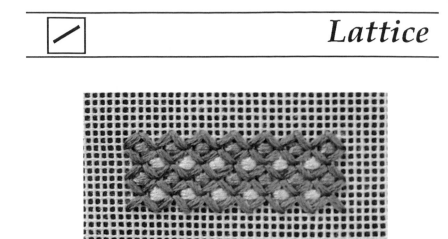

Lattice makes a neat two-colour stitch which can look like diamond paned windows if used on a house picture. It is quite time consuming to work and so should not be used for very large areas.

Follow the numbering carefully to get the correct sequence of stitches — notice that all the diagonal stitches which slope the same way in the row are worked first. The centre of the diamond is usually filled with an upright cross stitch, but three satin stitches may be used for a different effect.

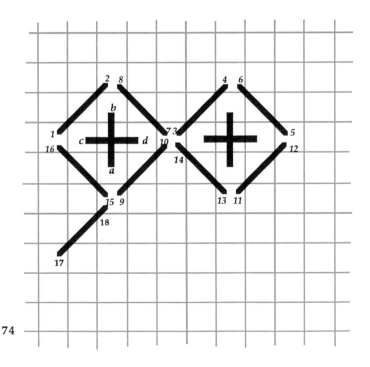

Milanese

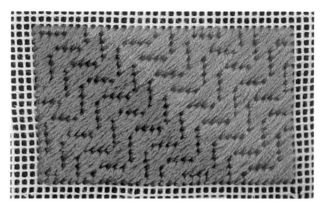

Milanese is a favourite stitch which is useful in many different kinds of needlepoint. It makes a very effective sky in a landscape, with many possibilities for shading, though it may distort the canvas if used over very large continuous areas. The wavy look which comes when quite an extensive area has been worked makes it suitable for water, and with its striking appearance it is invaluable in patterned pieces of work.

The stitch is worked over 1,2,3,4 canvas intersections and then repeated. The longest stitch of one row fits against the shortest stitch of the preceding row. Keep the tension even for best results. It is not always easy to work out the compensation stitches in Milanese, so it is often best to work a part of the row where the whole stitch fits in, and then go back to work the compensation stitches.

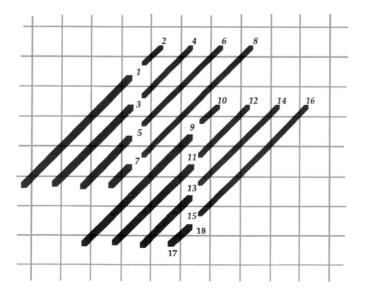

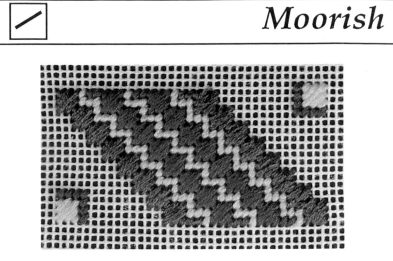

Moorish stitch is a bold diagonal stitch which if used over large areas will distort the canvas. It is made up of diagonal ground stitch with a line of tent stitch between each row. Thus the first row is made up of diagonal stitches over 1,2,3,2 canvas intersections and then repeated, while the next and alternate rows are stitched over just one intersection of the canvas.

Moorish stitch may be used to good effect in patterned pieces, using two or more colours, and can also be used in pictorial subjects in shades of the same colour.

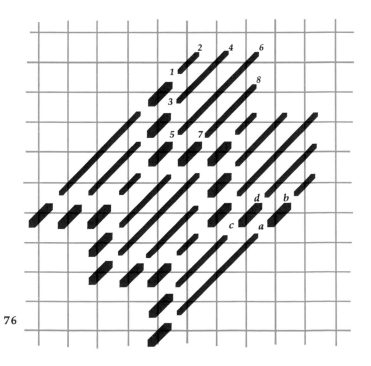

Mosaic

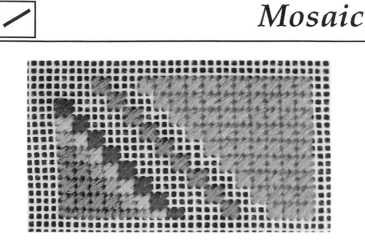

Although the finished stitch looks not unlike smooth lines of cross stitches, mosaic stitch is most easily worked diagonally, in groups of three stitches over 1,2,1 canvas intersections and then repeated. On the return row the long stitches fit into the gaps between the groups of stitches making up the first row. When viewed diagonally, the long stitches are all in line with each other, as are the short ones.

This is a neat, flat stitch, useful for patterned pieces of work, and as a foil for more sculptured stitches in pictures. Being small, it can be used in the background of landscapes, with larger, bolder stitches making up the foreground.

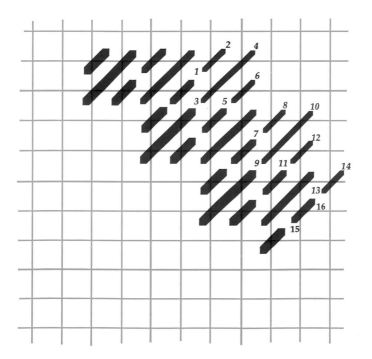

Mountain stitch was developed to give the effect of the varied planes visible on mountain sides — hence the name. It is used over large areas of the Waterfall and Tropical Rain Forest pictures (pp. 36 & 108).

Groups of long stitches are worked in various triangular shapes, the bases of the triangles being along horizontal or sloping lines and the tops being in a single hole or several adjacent holes. The top and bottom holes are often hidden underneath other groups of stitches and care must be taken not to split the threads of these other stitches.

The colours of the stitches in a group may be the same, mixed in the needle or mixed in the group, and the colours usually vary throughout the mountain side to give the effect of plays of light or snowy areas.

This type of stitchery, which has to be worked in an 'over and over' fashion, eats the thread and can look very messy on the back, but it is the only way to achieve these particular effects.

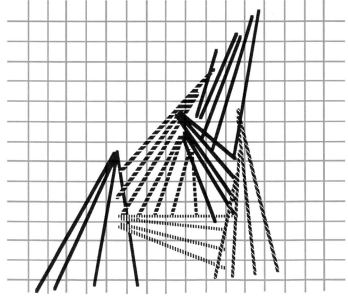

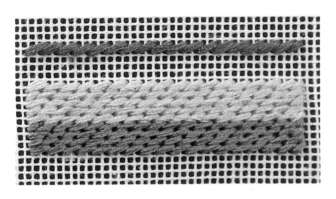

Oblique Slav stitch has a very smooth, gently sloping appearance and is worked in lines from left to right and back again.

Work from bottom to top of the area to be covered and turn the work upside down to work the return row if you find it easier.

Start by working a stitch over three vertical and one horizontal canvas threads. Bring the needle to the front again one canvas thread down and one thread back. Repeat the stitch to the end of the row. Turn the work if more convenient and start stitching again one thread back and one thread down, following the numbers on the diagram carefully.

This is a useful stitch for hillsides or neat backgrounds.

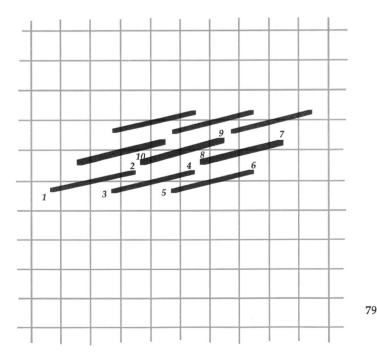

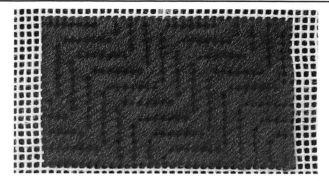

Oriental is a handsome stitch which must be used over a large area for the full effect to be appreciated. When worked in a single colour a large diagonal wave pattern gradually emerges. The stitch may also be worked in two colours, the pattern then looking completely different.

The first part of the stitch is worked over 1,2,3,4 canvas intersections, making arrowheads, and then repeated. Next, with either the same, or the second colour, stitches over two canvas intersections are worked up against all but the longest stitch of the previous row. The second row arrowheads point in the opposite direction from those in the first, the long stitches lining up with each other, unlike Milanese.

When adding compensation stitches, it is best to work a part of the row first where a whole stitch fits in. Then it is easy to see what the compensation stitches should be. Oriental is useful for skies, water, and in two colours in patterned pieces.

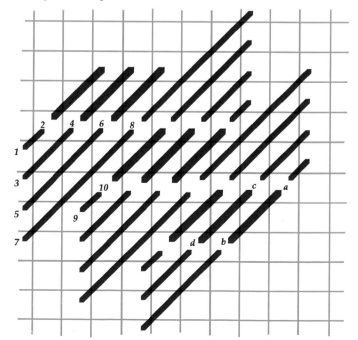

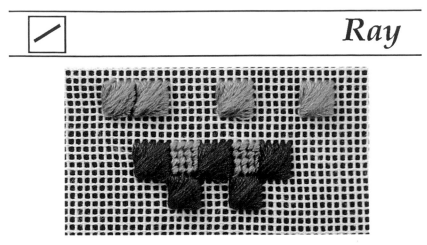

Ray is a more complex form of fan stitch, but because every hole around the square is filled, it is much more three-dimensional.

Bring the working thread out in the bottom left-hand corner of a square of four canvas threads. The first part of the stitch is taken across to the bottom right-hand corner over four canvas threads, the second stitch is taken up to the top left-hand corner and so on until the the final stitch is taken across the top of all the others from bottom left to top right. The hole used nine times may be first opened up slightly with a blunt needle or the ends of small scissors.

Ray stitches look very handsome if contrasted in a chequerboard pattern with squares of tent stitch. The rays may of course be stitched to face the opposite way. Ray stitch is not much used in pictorial work.

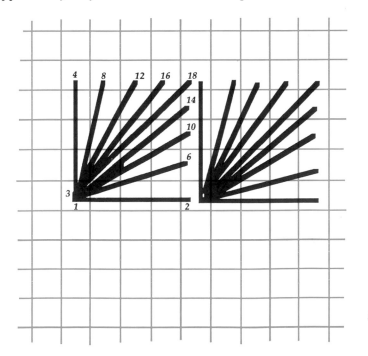

81

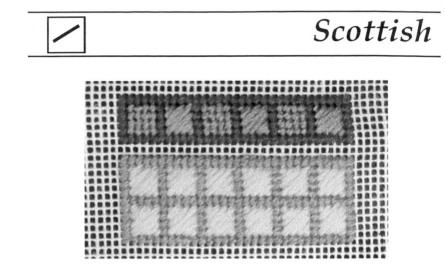

Scottish stitch is a composite stitch made up of squares outlined in tent stitch filled in chequerboard fashion with diagonal satin stitch and tent stitch. All the outlining boxes should be worked first. The stitches inside the boxes look best in a different colour from the outlining.

As a variation all the squares may be filled with diagonal satin stitch, possibly alternating the direction of the diagonal stitches, thus giving very attractive plays of light on the threads.

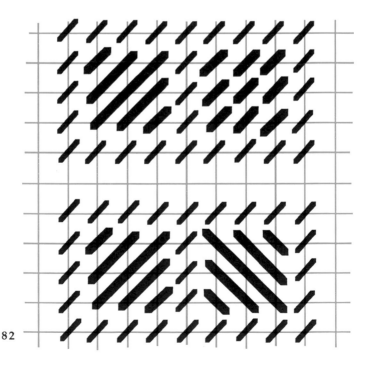

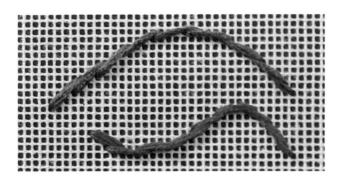

Sometimes it is difficult to achieve a smooth outline for a rounded feature because the square mesh of the canvas dictates where stitches are placed. In these cases the feature may be outlined in the same or a different colour, and for this either back stitch or stem stitch may be used. Stem stitch has a thicker but more curving line.

To look neat the stitches should be of similar length but may be taken in any direction, the needle being brought out half-way back along the stitch (either above or below depending on which direction the line is going), before starting the next stitch.

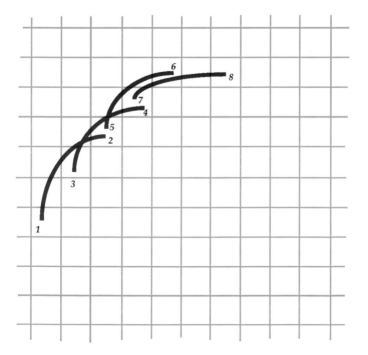

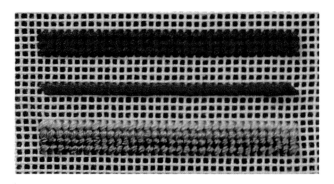

Tent is one of the basic needlepoint stitches and is made diagonally across one canvas intersection. It is easy to work this stitch wrongly by doing alternate rows of tent stitch and half cross stitch without realising. Try to remember that when working from left to right along the row, the actual stitch is worked from right to left and vice versa. Follow the numbering on the chart carefully. If you prefer, you may turn the work upside down to work the second and alternate rows, in which case the stitch is made in the same way each row. To check whether you are doing the correct stitch, look at the back of the work, which should be covered all over with rows of diagonal stitchery. The middle row of stitching on the picture above shows the *back* of the stitches.

Although strong and neat, continental tent has the disadvantage that it distorts the shape of the canvas. On most occasions therefore, it is preferable to use basketweave tent stitch.

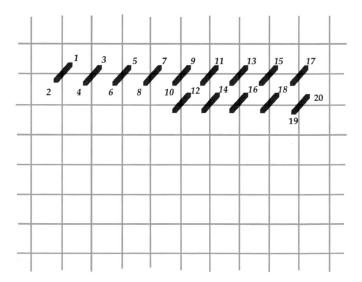

Basketweave Tent

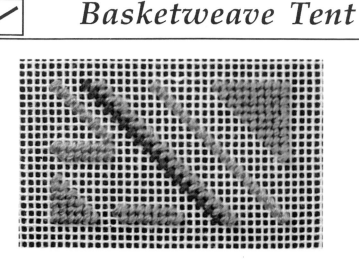

Basketweave tent stitch consists of diagonal stitches across one intersection of the canvas which are worked up and down diagonals. Owing to the opposing pull of the 'basketweave effect' stitches on the back of the work, no distortion is caused to the canvas. This is obviously an important factor if large areas are to be worked in this stitch.

When using basketweave, break off for rests in the middle of a row rather than at an end, so that you know which way along the diagonal you are working. The stitching may look uneven if you work two consecutive rows in the same direction.

The diagrams show how basketweave tent may be used in different shaped areas — even as a two-row horizontal or vertical stripe.

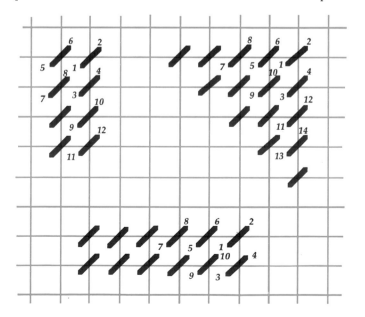

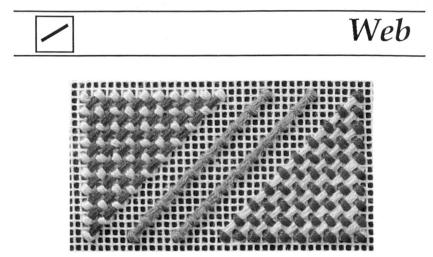

Web

Web stitch is worked in two stages, usually in two colours. Initially diagonal threads are laid across the canvas from every other hole down one edge. As each thread is laid, so it is tied down over every other intersection along its length, using a separate needle if a second colour is being used. On the adjacent rows the tying down threads are staggered, giving a woven appearance.

Web stitch is used mainly in patterned work.

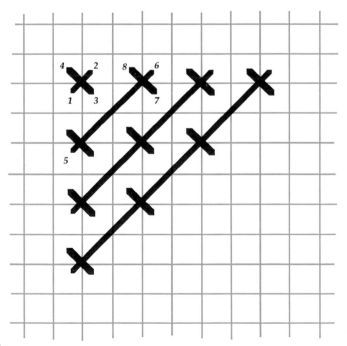

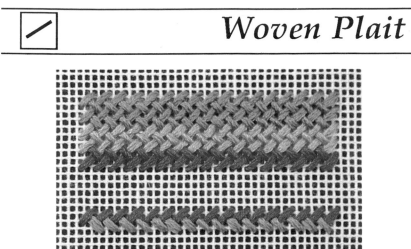

Woven plait is a small, neat and easily worked stitch which, having a definite diagonal interwoven effect, forms a good contrast with most other stitches. This makes it useful both in patterns and in pictorial designs. The lines may be worked all in the same colour, all in different colours or in shades of the same colour, depending on the effect required.

The first row is a line of diagonal stitches worked from left to right over two canvas intersections with two canvas threads between each stitch. The second row stitches, which may be worked from right to left, are also over two canvas intersections, the top of each stitch being placed in the hole covered by the stitches of the first row. You may have to push the thread aside with your needle to see the correct hole. Take care not to catch the threads of the first row stitches.

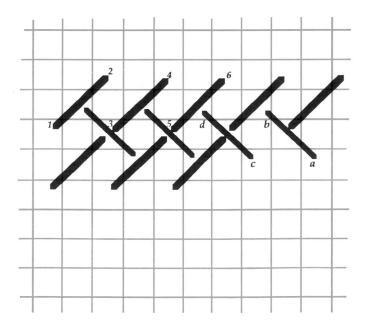

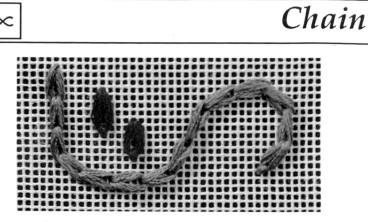

Chain stitch can be worked closely packed together in vertical lines from top to bottom of the canvas, in which case it resembles stocking stitch in knitting. There are however many needlepoint stitches which cover large areas of canvas easily and neatly, but few which can be worked round curves and laid in any direction across the canvas. As chain stitch is one of these few, it is most useful for work of this kind, especially since the stitches may be made any size required.

The stitches are made towards the worker. The needle and working thread are brought to the front of the canvas at the start of the chain. While a loop of thread is held down with the left thumb, the needle and thread are taken back into the original hole and out at the far end of the stitch, over the loop of thread being held down. Usually this is done all in one movement, but this is not necessary if a frame is being used. To finish off the chain the needle and thread are taken to the back of the work over the end of the last loop.

Chain stitch is useful for plant effects or letters and numbers worked on top of other stitchery.

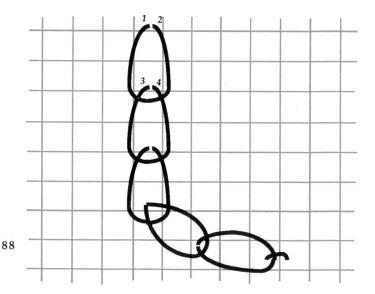

Needleweaving

∝

Needleweaving is used to make a leaf-shaped bar of close grained stitchery which is only attached to the canvas at each end. Thus it can be made any length and can lie in any direction on the canvas.

Firstly sew two firmly laid down stitches coming out of and going into the same hole at each end. Next bring the needle and working thread out of the first hole again and take it over the left-hand laid thread and under the right-hand laid thread. Then repeat the process in reverse, over the right-hand thread and under the left. Pull the whole thread through with each movement and maintain an even tension to keep the weaving neat. Pack the stitches closely to give the best effect.

Needleweaving may be used to give a truly three-dimensional aspect to floral and pictorial pieces of work.

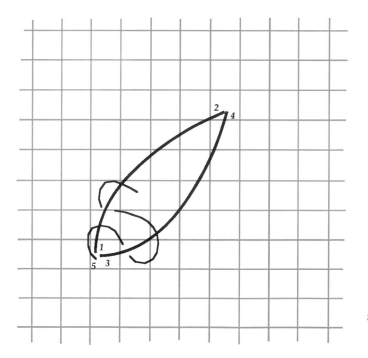

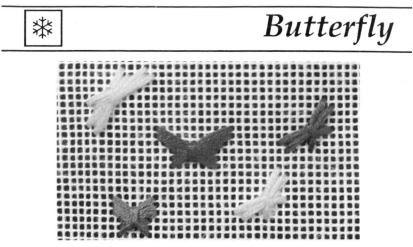

This pretty stitch may be used as a motif or as a butterfly in a picture. It is possible to work as either a straight or a diagonal stitch.

For the straight version, begin by working next to each other three vertical stitches over eight canvas threads, and three vertical stitches over six canvas threads. To find the correct hole to come up through for the binding, gently pull aside the longer threads with a fingernail and bring the needle right out through the middle hole underneath the third long thread. Slide the needle underneath the long threads on the front of the canvas, bring over the whole stitch, in again under the short threads and feel around for the same hole to take the needle to the back again. Pull the binding tightly.

The diagonal version makes a realistic butterfly shape for a picture, or may be set in a square of tent stitch in a patterned design. Work in a similar way to the straight version, following the diagram.

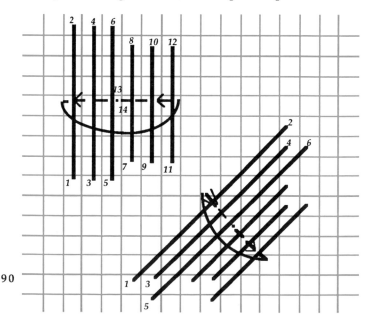

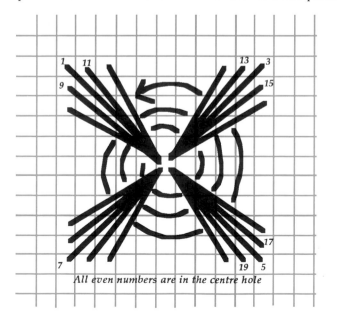

Petal is a handsome, three-dimensional stitch usually worked over a square of ten canvas threads and is best used as a single motif, although petals can be worked next to each other as a continuous background if required.

Before starting to stitch, open up the centre hole with a large needle. Into this hole from each corner make diagonal stitches across five canvas intersections. Place two more diagonal stitches into the centre hole from either side of each of the first four stitches as shown on the diagram.

With the same, or a different, colour bring the needle out one hole away from the centre, and carefully wind the thread five times round the centre, under the stitches already in place. Be careful not to catch any of the threads of the diagonal stitches. Take the needle to the back of the work behind a group of diagonal stitches. Tie down the outside ring at the centre point of each side with a back stitch as shown on the photograph.

All even numbers are in the centre hole

This cheerful turtle, worked by the author on 13s interlock canvas with crewel wools, has divisions on his shell which provide an ideal way of showing off various motif and leaf stitches.

The stitches used include spider's web, petal, leaf, wheel variation, scallop, Norwich, Rhodes and a graduated sheaf stitch ring. The head and legs are in diagonal mosaic, the background is the straight version of Oriental in two shades of misty turquoise, while the edging is two rows of long legged cross.

The inspiration for this turtle was a picture in a child's alphabet book which was redrawn to make it a suitable subject for needlepoint. The finished article could be framed as a picture or made into a cushion.

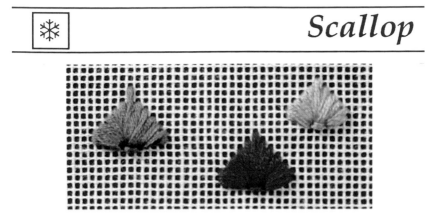

Scallop is a useful motif stitch in that it may be done in different sizes to meet the needs of the occasion. It usually has a decidedly three-dimensional quality, but if this is not desired, the number of strands of thread in the needle may be reduced. Its main uses are in formal patterned pieces of work, where several may be placed against a background of tent stitch, or single scallops may be used as corner motifs.

The stitch is worked from three holes at the base and has a triangular top. On the scallop illustrated the outside stitches are made over four vertical and one horizontal canvas threads, while the middle (tallest) stitch may be made over seven or eight horizontal canvas threads, depending on how pointed the scallop is required. Four stitches are placed in the outer holes and five in the middle hole.

The motif is finished off with a small horizontal straight stitch across the base of the other stitches.

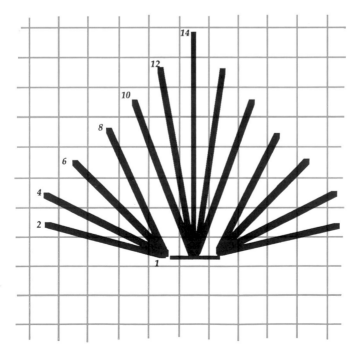

Satin Flower

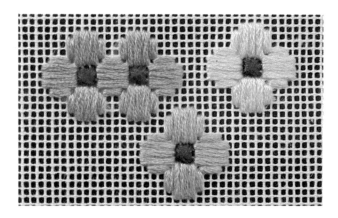

These satin stitch flowers look very pretty scattered over a tent stitch background, possibly in a variety of colours, or they can be stitched as a continuous border of flower heads round a geometrical design. Alternatively, just one flower can be used as a motif.

The flowers may be stitched in two different sizes. The larger has petals made up of stitches over 3,5,5,5,3 canvas threads, each petal being stitched at right angles to the two on either side. A smaller petal made over 2,4,4,4,2 canvas threads may also be used for the flower.

The centre of the flower is finished with a Smyrna cross over a square of two threads.

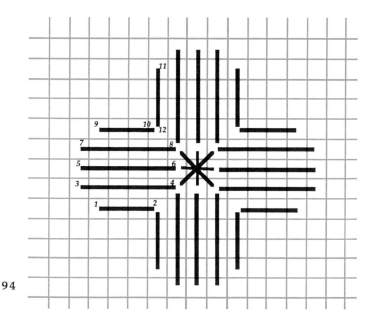

Snowflake is a motif stitch, made up by a student of the author, and is ideal for use on needlework Christmas cards.

It is best worked in two or three colours, unless you require a traditional white snowflake on a darker background. It is very simple, being composed of straight and back stitches at various angles, apart from four French knots which decorate the corners.

Follow the numbering and lettering on the diagram for working instructions.

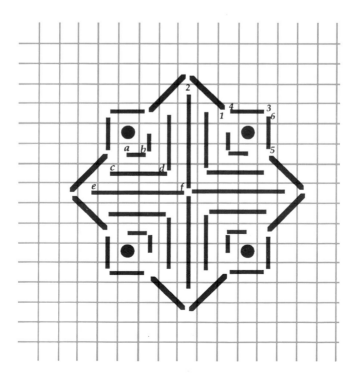

95

Spider's web is a round, three-dimensional stitch which is very useful for all sorts of special effects. Although they may be grouped together, spiders' webs are really motif stitches and show up best on their own against a flatter background. They are equally useful in patterned designs or landscapes.

1. Work the basic framework of eight stitches into the central hole, keeping a firm tension.

2. Bring the needle out near the centre between any two of the legs. The rest of the stitch is worked on the surface of the canvas.

3. Take the needle and thread back over one leg and forward under two, keeping the centre hole towards you and turning the work, making sure not to catch any of the threads. Pull the stitches in towards the centre.

4. Keep working round in this way until the whole web is filled.

5. Take the needle through to the back of the canvas and fasten off.

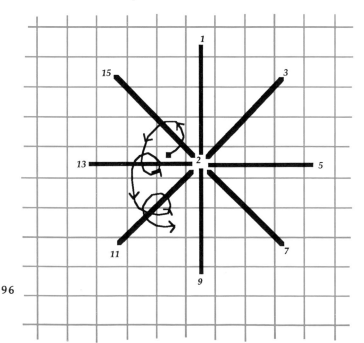

❄

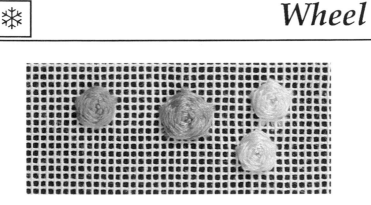

Wheel stitch makes a very three-dimensional round feature rather like a fabric button.

A five-armed star framework is laid down first, as shown on the diagram. This must be very firm so that it will stay in place as the wheel is built up. The working thread is brought to the front between any two of the arms near the centre, and is then threaded under and over alternate arms (on the surface of the canvas), and pulled in towards the centre. Continue until no more circuits can be made.

The three-dimensional nature of the wheel is governed by the number of times you go round, so for a very high wheel, add another circuit or two. To finish, push the needle through to the back of the work and fasten off.

Wheels are very useful motif stitches in pictures where they can represent flowers, bushes or other features.

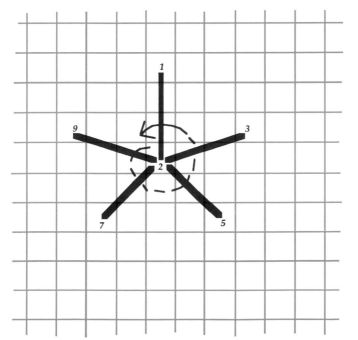

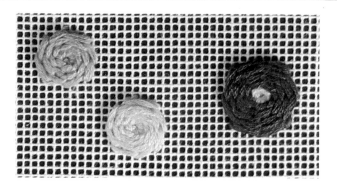

Wheel variation has a flatter top and sides than wheel stitch itself, but is similar in that it makes a very three-dimensional round motif.

Lay down an eight-arm framework, as in spider's web stitch, on which to build up the wheel. The framework must be firm so that it will not move when being worked on.

Bring the needle and working thread out between any two arms as near to the centre as possible, but not through the middle hole. Then take the needle and thread forward over two arms and back under one, on the surface of the canvas, repeating this until the wheel is the size required. The more times the thread is taken round the wheel the more it will build up. It is easier to work this stitch if you move the canvas round as you work and keep pulling the thread gently in towards the centre.

These wheels may be used to represent various features on pictures and to create points of interest on patterned pieces.

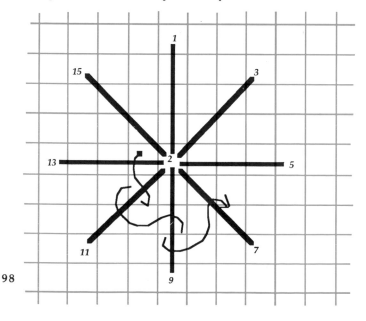

H

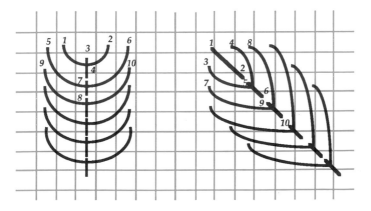

Fly stitch consists of a very firm V-shaped line of stitching held down with small straight stitches. It can make a very dense background, or a single line of straight fly may be used effectively as a tree trunk or other upright feature. Diagonal fly makes flowers, leaves or ears of corn.

To begin the top of the straight stitch bring the needle through to the front of the work. Holding the thread under the left thumb, push the needle into the hole two threads to the right and bring it out to the front again in one movement through the hole one row down, between the two holes already used. Make sure the needle comes out above the loop of thread under the left thumb, so that when the thread is pulled tight, the loop is held down and can then be tied down with a small vertical stitch into the hole immediately below. The second and succeeding stitches are made in the same way, but are wider and deeper, having four vertical canvas threads between the two top stitches and two horizontal canvas threads between where the needle goes in at the top right and comes out in the middle hole below. The second stitch is started at the same level as the first, and succeeding stitches one row down.

Diagonal fly is worked in a similar manner. Follow the numbering carefully and you will find these stitches are easier than they sound.

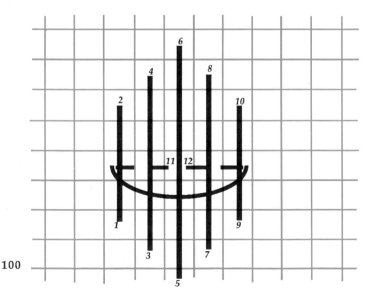

Graduated Sheaf

This is a most striking and versatile stitch which is equally useful in formal patterned designs and landscape pictures. It can be worked either vertically or horizontally and in two different sizes, as well as being used to form other composite stitches.

1. Lay down the straight stitches forming the basic framework of the stitch over 4,6,8,6,4 horizontal canvas threads.
2. Find the middle hole under the longest stitch by moving the stitch aside with a fingernail. Pull the needle and thread through to the front.
3. Slide the needle and thread under the threads at one side, across the front and under the threads at the other side. Then take back down the centre hole to the back, 'binding' the sheaf by pulling tightly.

A smaller sheaf may be worked over 2,4,6,4,2 canvas threads.

Four sheaves interlocked at right angles to each other make a beautiful ring which can be filled with tent stitch in the same or a different colour. Sheaves can also be placed under each other and others interlocked alongside them to form features such as trees.

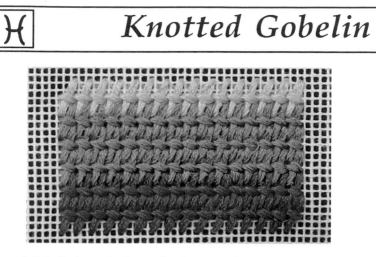

Knotted Gobelin is worked over five horizontal and two vertical canvas threads. The knotting or tying-down stitch is worked slanting across the centre of this sloping stitch over one horizontal and two vertical canvas threads, as shown on the diagram. The placing of this knotting stitch may seem a little difficult on the first row, but on succeeding rows it is easier because it goes into the bottom of the long stitches of the row above. Two canvas threads must be left between each long stitch so that the top of the long stitch of the row below can be fitted into the space.

This stitch makes a firm textured surface, which with its attractive slanting appearance is equally useful in pictorial or patterned subjects.

The colour may be varied between the rows for either a striped or shaded effect.

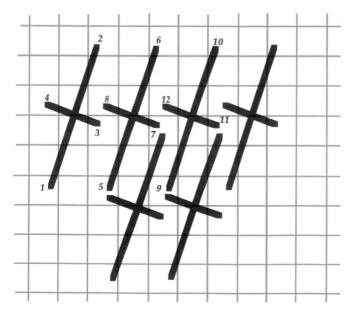

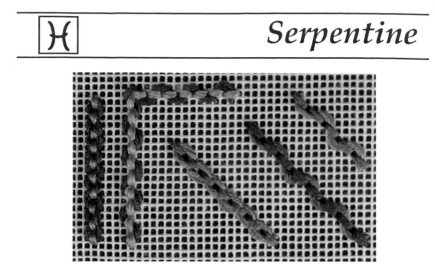

Serpentine stitch is worked on a base of back stitch, and thus can be made at any angle on the canvas. To achieve an even look to the stitch the back stitches of the base should be of the same size.

Firstly work a row of back stitches where the serpentine is required. Bring a contrasting coloured thread to the front of the work and weave it through the back stitches on the surface of the canvas from alternate directions, as shown in the picture and on the diagram.

In double serpentine the contrasting thread is taken through the back stitches twice, making loops on both sides of the original line of stitching.

Serpentine may be used to create a piped effect round the edges of pieces of work. It can also be worked on top of a background of any smooth stitch to create a sculptured design.

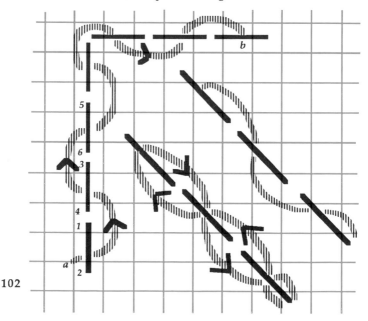

102

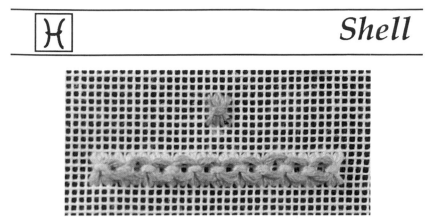

To begin shell stitch four vertical stitches are made over four canvas threads, not necessarily in an over-and-over fashion (see numbering). Next bring the needle to the front of the work through the middle hole to the left of the central canvas thread, and tie the laid threads together like a sheaf by taking the working thread over the group and to the back again through the middle hole to the right of the central canvas thread.

A line of such groups is made and then a contrasting thread is threaded through the 'ties' twice so that there appears to be a chain lying on top of the original groups of stitches. This contrasting threading must be carefully done to keep an even appearance.

Shell stitch can look highly decorative, especially if in addition a bead is sewn into each resulting hole, but has the disadvantage of being easily caught and is therefore not suitable for a piece of work which will receive much wear.

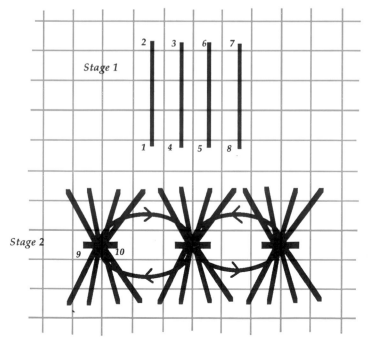

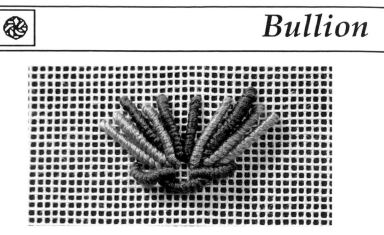

Bullion stitch looks rather like an elongated French knot lying on the canvas, and is very useful in pictorial work as it can be worked in any direction and to any length within reason.

The needle and a long working thread are brought out to the front of the canvas at 1 (one end of the bullion stitch) and taken down again at 2 (the other end of the stitch), leaving the thread loose in between. Bring the needle point only out again at 1 and wind the loose thread round the needle a sufficient number of times to fill the space between points 1 and 2. Hold the twists with the left hand while working the needle and thread through them. Still holding the twists in place on the thread, take the needle through to the back of the work at 2. Arrange the twists neatly with the point of the needle.

Groups of bullion stitches may be placed to depict roses, bushes or other features.

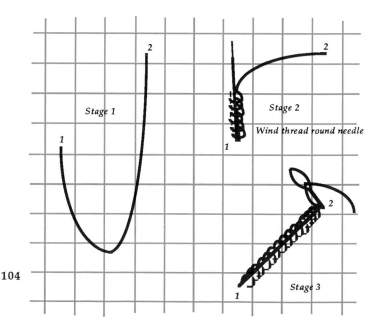

Stage 1

Stage 2
Wind thread round needle

Stage 3

The Danish knot may be used as an alternative to the French knot, though it is squarer in character. Some students find the French knot difficult to work, yet are perfectly happy with this Danish equivalent, so try both and see which suits you better.

The first part of the knot is a small diagonal stitch over one intersection of the canvas from bottom right to top left. Bring out the working thread in the hole below the top of this stitch and work two loops round the stitch as shown in the diagram. The needle is then taken to the back of the work to the right of the top of the original stitch.

Danish knots may be used to cover bare canvas or be placed over already worked areas to add depth. They can represent bushes and trees or gravel in pictures, as well as clouds, while in patterned pieces they may be used to fill whole areas.

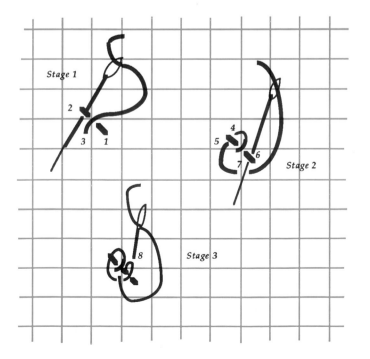

French knots are very easy to work once you know exactly how to hold the thread, and are among the most useful stitches in the needlepoint repertoire. They can be used singly as flowers, bunched tightly together to form any shape at all, from a tree to a cat, used to simulate a gravel path or added to many other stitches such as leaf stitch and Chinese fan stitch to add interest. Whole pieces of work may be done in knots.

The knot is worked as shown in the diagram.

1. Anchor the thread firmly on the back of the work and bring the needle and all the thread through to the front of the work where the knot is required.

2. Hold the thread fairly taut with your left hand about 1" away from the canvas. Twist the needle round the taut thread once (small knot), or twice (large knot).

3. Twist the needle with the thread round it down towards the canvas and insert into any of the adjacent holes - preferably not one across an intersection of the canvas threads. Make sure the knot is resting on the canvas and pull the needle through to the back. This gives a neat knot.

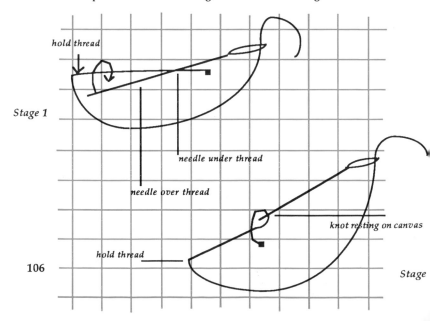

hold thread

Stage 1

needle under thread

needle over thread

knot resting on canvas

hold thread

Stage

French knots on stalks are very useful for the centres of flowers, and in the same way as ordinary French knots are very versatile, in this case because the stalk may be made almost any length, and the knot on the end any size within reason.

Proceed as follows:

1. Anchor the thread firmly on the back of the work and pull the needle and all the thread through to the front where you want the end of the stalk to be.

2. Hold the thread firmly with your left hand about 1" away from the canvas.

3. Wind the needle round the taut thread twice or three times.

4. With the thread still round the needle, position the needle in the hole where you want the knot to be, making sure the knot is resting on the canvas and the stalk is taut.

5. Pull the needle gently through the hole.

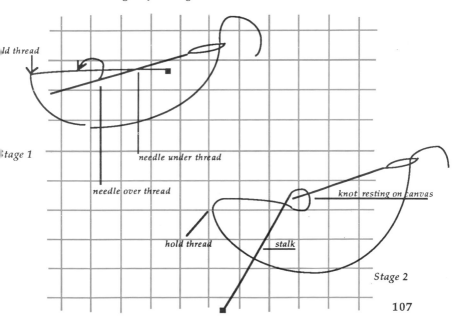

ld thread

Stage 1

needle under thread

needle over thread

knot resting on canvas

hold thread

stalk

Stage 2

107

Tropical Rain Forest needlepoint picture worked by the author in a variety of stitches. It was worked on 13s interlock canvas with crewel wools. The original idea for this picture came from a painting by Keith Grant. The picture measures 14" x 14" (35.5 x 35.5 cm).

Detail of palm tree and red flowers

Detail of mountain and cloud

108

Key to numbering on chart.

1. An enlarged leaf stitch was made first and built up to the required shape with straight stitches.
2. Twill stitch worked diagonally from top left to bottom right, pale blue and white threads mixed in the needle.
3. French knots, mostly white and cream, some with blue mixed in.
4. Mountain stitch with various blues and greys mixed in the needle.
5. Hungarian diamonds, white mixed with kingfisher.
6. Satin flowers.
7. Lines of stem stitches packed closely together.
8. Tightly packed French knots, red and putty coloured threads variously mixed in the needle.
9. Large spiders' webs on a background of tent stitch.
10. Centre of flower is French knots on stalks.
11. Various coloured petal stitches.
12. Trunk of the palm tree is straight fly stitch.
13. Background is random jacquard stitch in shades of olive brown and gold.
14. Grasses are stem stitches in various greens and browns.
15. Tiger is random straight stitches in tigerish colours.

List of stitches by type

Straight Stitches
Arrowhead 12
Back 13
Brick 14
Single Brick 16
Double Brick 17
Chevron 18
Diamond Straight 19
Florentine 20
Hungarian 21
Hungarian Diamonds 22
Hungarian Grounding 23
Indian Stripe 24
Long 25
Straight Oriental 26
Parisian & Small Parisian 27
Satin 28
Satin Square 29
Single Trammed Gobelin 30
Tramming 31
Triangle 32
Twill & Double Twill 33
Water 34
Waterfall 35
Weaving 38
Willow 39

Crossed Stitches
Cross 40
Single Cross 41
Double Cross 42
Smyrna Cross 43
Upright Cross 44
Fern 45
Crossed Gobelin 46
Double Leviathan 47
Long Legged Cross & Long
 Legged Cross Variation 48
Norwich 49
Rhodes 50
Rice (Crossed Corners) 52

Eyelet Stitches
Algerian Eye 53
Diamond Eyelet 54
Octagonal Eye 55

Pile Stitches
Turkish Knot 57
Velvet 58

Leaf Stitches
Chinese Fan 59
Leaf 60
Leaf Square 61
Leaf Variations 62

Diagonal Stitches
Brighton 63
Byzantine 64
Cashmere 65
Cushion 66
Diagonal Ground 67
Diagonal Mosaic 69
Fan 70
Gobelin 71
Half Cross 72
Jacquard 73
Lattice 74
Milanese 75
Moorish 76
Mosaic 77
Mountain 78
Oblique Slav 79
Oriental 80
Ray 81
Scottish 82
Stem 83
Continental Tent 84
Basketweave Tent 85
Web 86
Woven Plait 87

Looped Stitches
Chain 88
Needleweaving 89

Motif Stitches
Butterfly 90
Petal 91
Satin Flower 94
Scallop 93
Snowflake 95
Spider's Web 96
Wheel 97
Wheel Variation 98

Tied Stitches
Fly & Diagonal Fly 99
Graduated Sheaf 100
Knotted Gobelin 101
Serpentine & Double
 Serpentine 102
Shell 103

Knot Stitches
Bullion 104
Danish Knot 105
French Knot 106
French Knot on Stalk 107

Alphabetical list of stitches

Algerian eye 53
Arrowhead 12

Back 13
Brick 14
Brick, double 17
Brick, single 16
Brighton 63
Bullion 104
Butterfly 90
Byzantine 64

Cashmere 65
Chevron 18
Chain 88
Chinese fan 59
Cross 40
Cross, double 42
Cross, long legged 48
Cross, single 41
Cross, Smyrna 43
Cross, upright 44
Cushion 66

Danish knot 105
Diagonal ground 67
Diamond straight 19

Eyelet, diamond 54

Fan 70
Fern 45
Fly 99
Florentine 20
French knot 106
French knot on a stalk 107

Gobelin 71
Gobelin, crossed 46
Gobelin, knotted 101
Gobelin, single trammed 30
Graduated sheaf 100

Half cross 72
Hungarian 21
Hungarian diamonds 22
Hungarian grounding 23

Indian stripe 24

Jacquard 73

Lattice 74
Leaf 60
Leaf square 61

Leaf variations 62
Leviathan, double 47
Long 25

Milanese 75
Moorish 76
Mosaic 77
Mosaic, diagonal 69
Mountain 78

Needleweaving 89
Norwich 49

Oblique Slav 79
Octagonal eye 55
Oriental 80
Oriental, straight 26

Parisian 27
Petal 91

Ray 81
Rhodes 50
Rice 52

Satin 28
Satin flower 94
Satin square 29
Scallop 93
Scottish 82
Serpentine 102
Shell 103
Snowflake 95
Stem 83
Spider's web 96

Tent, basketweave 85
Tent, continental 84
Tramming 31
Triangle 32
Turkish knot 57
Twill 33

Velvet 58

Water 34
Waterfall 35
Weaving 38
Web 86
Wheel 97
Wheel variation 98
Willow 39
Woven plait 87

Bibliography & Suppliers

Christensen, Jo Ippolito *The Needlepoint Book,* New York 1986

Good Housekeeping *Needlepoint,* London 1981

Gray, Jennifer *Canvas Work,* London 1955

Hanley, Hope *101 Needlepoint Stitches & how to use them,* New York 1986

Kurten, Nancy N. *Needlepoint: Stitch by Stitch,* New York 1977

Rhodes, Mary *Dictionary of Canvas Work Stitches,* London 1980

Suppliers of Madeira Threads

UNITED KINGDOM

A full list of suppliers in the United Kingdom and other English-speaking countries is available on request from Madeira Threads (UK) Ltd, Thirsk Industrial Park, York Road, Thirsk, North Yorkshire YO7 3BX.

EUROPE

Madeira Garne
U. & M. Schmidt & Co. GmbH
Hans Buntestr 8
D-7800 FREIBURG
WEST GERMANY

Kasite Ky
Hameentie 4C 10
00530 HELSINKI
FINLAND

USA

Madeira USA Ltd
30 Bayside Court
LACONIA
New Hampshire 03246

Madeira USA Ltd (West Coast)
2727 N. Grove Industrial Drive
FRESNO
California 93727

AUSTRALIA
Penguin Threads Pty Ltd
25-27 Izett Street
PRAHAN 3181
Victoria